Stotra Series : 2

Prayer Guide

(with explanations of several Mantras,
Stotras, Kirtans,
and Religious Festivals)

Swami Dayananda Saraswati
Arsha Vidya

Arsha Vidya
Research and Publication Trust
Chennai

Published by :
Arsha Vidya Research
and Publication Trust
32 / 4 ' Sri Nidhi ' Apts III Floor
Sir Desika Road Mylapore
Chennai 600 004 INDIA
Tel : 044 2499 7023
Telefax: 2499 7131
Email : avrandpc@gmail.com

ISBN : 978 - 81 - 906059 - 1 - 5

First Edition	: October	2008	Copies : 1000
1st Reprint	: May	2009	Copies : 2000

Design :
Suchi Ebrahim

Printed by :
Sudarsan Graphics
27, Neelakanta Mehta Street
T. Nagar, Chennai 600 017
Email : info@sudarsan.com

Contents

Preface ix

Key to Transliteration xi

Understanding Prayer

Need for Prayer 1

Action is *mithyā* 2

Control of hidden variables 4

Our free will is not that 'free' 5

Following *dharma* helps us 'become' free 7

Prayer is the only 'completely free' action on the part of a *kartṛ* 11

Primarily prayer is for *adṛṣṭa-phala*, unseen result 12

The world is a manifestation of Īśvara 15

Conforming to *dharma* is being in harmony with Īśvara 16

Prayer produces *puṇya* 19

Śāstra reveals the existence of *adṛṣṭa-phala* 21

Human life is a mixture of *puṇya* and *pāpa* 22

Ritualistic Prayer

Śrauta-karma 29

Smārta-karma 30

Ritualistic prayer produces the maximum *puṇya* 31
Altars 32

Oral Prayer
All names are Īśvara's names 34
You can invoke Īśvara in a particular name 36

Mental Prayer
Meditation is mental activity focused on Īśvara 40
Japa 43
Japa helps train our mind 45
Mind is but an instrument 47
Significance of 108 48
Prayerfulness 49

Devotion
Becoming a devotee 50
The lord is the creator and I am the created 52
Relationship with Īśvara is crucial to one's becoming a devotee 54
Pūjā 54
Altar of worship 57
Meditation 58
Love has to be discovered 59
Pūjā helps us gain *jñāna* 60
Akhaṇḍa-nāma-japa 60
Three types of *japa* 61
Akhaṇḍa-japa transforms you 61

Mantra Initiation

Mantra initiation is also for girls 64
Initiation before teenage years 65
Make your vows public 66
Father initiates son into the *mantra* in *upanayana* 67
Japa becomes an inner guide for the initiated 67
Initiation 69
Count by time 69
Every committed person is eligible for a *mantra* 69

Forms of Worship

Everything is sacred 73
Worshipping a form is a blessing 74
Lord Gaṇeśa 74
Lord Naṭarāja 75
Śrī Dakṣiṇāmūrti 77
The Lord as the eight aspects 77
The Lord as the teacher 79
Śivaliṅga 81
Worship of the Five Elements 82

Mantras and Stotras

Śuklāmbaradharam 85
Agajānana-padmārkam 87
Yā kundendu 89
Gāyatrī-mantra 91
Oṁ namo bhagavate dakṣiṇāmūrtaye 95
Maunavyākhyā 97

Nidhaye sarvavidyānām 100
Oṁ namaḥ praṇavārthāya 101
Īśvaro gururātmeti 102
Tatpuruṣāya vidmahe 103
Rājādhirājāya 105
Na tatra sūryo bhāti 108
Śrīrāma rāma rāmeti 110
Namaste astu bhagavan 111
Śivamānasapūjā 114
Saha nāvavatu 127

Om

Om as a word 131
Om as a sound-symbol 133
Praṇava, om, is only for *sannyāsins* 137

Overview of Rudram and Camakam

In Camakam we ask the Lord to give us everything 138
The Lord is the order that sustains everything 140
Recognising the order helps reduce our subjectivity 141
Our subjectivity is part of the order 142
Chanting Rudram reduces our subjectivity 143
The vision of oneness 144
Rudram and Camakam are complementary 145
In the Lord's vision everything is in order 145

The Gist of Puruṣa Sūktam

Description of the *puruṣa* 148

All beings are the *puruṣa* 150

Chanting Puruṣa Sūktam regularly neutralises the sense of ownership 150

The Lord can be recognised in the heart 154

The Lord is everything 155

He is the lord of time and of all the worlds 156

Introduction to Viṣṇusahasranāma

Why so many names? 157

A *stotra* is meaningful only when it comes from a wise person 159

A word and its meaning are inseparable 161

Three sets of words:

Svarūpa names 162

Guṇa names 163

Līlā names 165

Invoke the Lord's grace through prayer 166

Seek help from one who does not need help 167

Pūrṇa-kumbha mantra 168

Paramānanda is attained by renunciation 171

Ignorance veils the Lord's presence in the intellect 172

The *sannyāsins* committed to knowledge 'gain' *paramānanda* 174

How do they gain this knowledge? 174

Such *sannyāsins* are totally liberated 177

Kirtans

Vandehaṁ śāradām 183
Dakṣiṇāmūrte amūrte 189
The world is like a tree 190
The Lord as the *guru* 193
Khelati mama hṛdaye 195

Religious Festivals

Sarasvatī pūjā 199
Everything is sacred 200
Navarātri festival in Tamil Nadu 201
Rāmanavamī 202
Śivarātri 221
Lord Śiva is auspiciousness 221
Lord Śiva is the lord of time 222
Gurupūrṇimā 225
Cāturmāsya-vrata 225
A *guru* unfolds spiritual knowledge 226
We invoke the Lord in the *guru* 228
Knowing implies removal of inhibiting factors 231
The teaching method 236
Śrī Śaṅkara Jayanti 238
Śrī Śaṅkarācārya as *upādhi-viśeṣa* 240
Śrī Śaṅkarācārya and the teaching tradition, *sampradāya* 245

Preface

This is a very useful book consisting of independent topics under one title 'Prayer Guide'. A given topic may be a discussion on a verse that one may be chanting daily, or a word that needs to be understood thoroughly.

Over a period of time I had talked on different occasions like *Guru-pūrṇima, Śaṅkara-jayanti* and so on, and they are all here; each is found strengthening a weak link in our total understanding. Therefore, I consider this book will be found useful to every reader. I enjoyed my reading and re-editing this book.

Swami Dayananda Saraswati
Arsha Vidya
September 04 2008

Key to Transliteration and Pronunciation of Sanskrit Letters

Sanskrit is a highly phonetic language and hence accuracy in articulation of the letters is important. For those unfamiliar with the *Devanāgari* script, the international transliteration is a guide to the proper pronunciation of Sanskrit letters.

अ	*a*	*(but)*	ट	*ṭa*	*(true)**3
आ	*ā*	*(father)*	ठ	*ṭha*	*(anthill)**3
इ	*i*	*(it)*	ड	*ḍa*	*(drum)**3
ई	*ī*	*(beat)*	ढ	*ḍha*	*(godhead)**3
उ	*u*	*(full)*	ण	*ṇa*	*(under)**3
ऊ	*ū*	*(pool)*	त	*ta*	*(path)**4
ऋ	*ṛ*	*(rhythm)*	थ	*tha*	*(thunder)**4
ॠ	*ṝ*	*(marine)*	द	*da*	*(that)**4
ऌ	*ḷ*	*(revelry)*	ध	*dha*	*(breathe)**4
ए	*e*	*(play)*	न	*na*	*(nut)**4
ऐ	*ai*	*(aisle)*	प	*pa*	*(put)* 5
ओ	*o*	*(go)*	फ	*pha*	*(loophole)**5
औ	*au*	*(loud)*	ब	*ba*	*(bin)* 5
क	*ka*	*(seek)* 1	भ	*bha*	*(abhor)**5
ख	*kha*	*(blockhead)**1	म	*ma*	*(much)* 5
ग	*ga*	*(get)* 1	य	*ya*	*(loyal)*
घ	*gha*	*(log hut)**1	र	*ra*	*(red)*
ङ	*ṅa*	*(sing)* 1	ल	*la*	*(luck)*
च	*ca*	*(chunk)* 2	व	*va*	*(vase)*
छ	*cha*	*(catch him)**2	श	*śa*	*(sure)*
ज	*ja*	*(jump)* 2	ष	*ṣa*	*(shun)*
झ	*jha*	*(hedgehog)**2	स	*sa*	*(so)*
ञ	*ña*	*(bunch)* 2	ह	*ha*	*(hum)*

ं	*ṁ*	*anusvāra*	(nasalisation of preceding vowel)
:	*ḥ*	*visarga*	(aspiration of preceding vowel)
*			No exact English equivalents for these letters

1.	Guttural	–	Pronounced from throat
2.	Palatal	–	Pronounced from palate
3.	Lingual	–	Pronounced from cerebrum
4.	Dental	–	Pronounced from teeth
5.	Labial	–	Pronounced from lips

The 5th letter of each of the above class – called nasals – are also pronounced nasally.

Understanding Prayer

Need for prayer

Every individual is both the agent of an action, *kartṛ*, as well as the one who experiences the result of an action, *bhoktṛ*. The result may be of an action done either recently or in the remote past, or even in previous lives. The *kartṛ* and the *bhoktṛ* are the same individual. As a doer one chooses to perform an action for a result, and as an enjoyer one experiences the result. One performs an action in order to enjoy the desired result of the action. Therefore, one is a *kartṛ* in order to be a *bhoktṛ*.

The problem here is, the *kartṛ* cannot completely determine the outcome. If that were so, every *karma* we do would produce what we want. However, the *kartṛ* is like a baseball player who swings the bat; sometimes connects and many a time does not. The one who has a better average in striking the ball is considered to be successful, still it is a percentage game. Our entire life is like that. This creates a certain helplessness felt by the individual. One plans in order to achieve one thing, but what one achieves may be quite different and sometimes even be the opposite, like the dot.com stock investments. One would be considered foolish if one did not invest one's money in a bullmarket of high-tech stocks. People who had safe portfolios invested in high-tech stocks;

some of them lost their entire life's savings. What we understand from this is that one can plan and do one's homework, and do what is to be done, but one cannot predict the outcome.

Action is mithyā

Action, *kriyā*, is one of the most interesting forms of *mithyā*.[1] You cannot identify a particular action as the one that produces a given result. Still you think that certain action produces certain result. The truth is that every action is a composite of a series of actions. Cooking is considered an action, but it consists of a series of actions. The sum total of the series of actions is considered to be the given action that produces a given result. Any given action consists of multiple actions in which every action is momentary. The action now done is gone for good. Then there is another action, and another action, and yet another. Thus, action can be split into so many actions, each of which is *kṣaṇika*, momentary, immediately disappearing into the past. When the action is momentary, the sum, *samūha*, of all these momentary actions is not there at all. Where is the *samūha*? There is no *samūha*. The sum does not exist because you can only sum up things that

---

[1] *Mithyā* is an ontological term to indicate a reality that has no independent existence. A clay pot, for instance, has no existence apart from clay, and therefore, with respect to the clay, is *mithyā* in terms of its reality.

are available. Everything that was done goes into the past. Therefore, Bhartṛhari in his *Vākyapadīya* (3-8-4) defines an action as: *guṇa-bhūtairavayavaiḥ samūhaḥ krama-janmanām.*

Every action is *guṇa-bhūta,* meant to produce a result. When you want to hammer a nail, it is one type of action, which has its own *guṇa,* its own attribute or property. If you want to pull out the nail, then you need a different type of action. There are many actions in each of these action. *Krama-janmanām* means a sequence, a series of action one after the other. It is a series of action that result in the so-called single action. The sum of their components, *avayava,* is what Bhartṛhari calls a *kriyā,* action.

When not all the actions in the series are available, since they are momentary, how then are we going to see their aggregate, the *samūha*? We do see because we have a *buddhi.* What is superimposed by our *buddhi* is called an action, *buddhyā prakalpitā kriyā iti vibhāṣyate.* It is superimposed with the help of memory. Each action that has gone before gets registered in our memory, and all of them together are assembled as one action. This is called *karma.* This is where we require Īśvara; else there is no accounting for the result of action, *karmaphala.* This is order, the cause-effect order, the action-reaction order. The order itself is Īśvara's *māyā.* Therefore, it is impossible to figure out all that is necessary to achieve a result.

Control of hidden variables

Every action is based on my knowledge of means and ends. This is the end I want to achieve; these would be the means to achieving that end, and I employ the means. This again is knowledge. But then, there are so many hidden variables over which I have no control. Between one momentary action and another momentary action, anything can happen, a heart attack, an accident, or a natural disaster. Even the means that I employ to achieve an end need not be the correct means. Sometimes as an agent, *kartṛ*, I can undergo a problem, or the action, *kriyā*, itself meets with an obstacle. Thus, there are many factors over which I have no control at all.

The human being does not have the power to control even the known variables; there are so many parameters and so many instructions to follow. In a litigious country like America, we follow so many procedures to accomplish what we want to accomplish. This is a highly instructed and guided society that makes every effort to try and control the known variables. Wherever we go, we are instructed. At the airport, there are so many signs instructing us to go up, go down, turn this way, and so on. Sometimes they are confusing. In the mind of the person who designed the arrow, it is very clear, but not so for others! These are all known variables. Yet with all these controls, to avoid any mishap, sometimes the wrong person is operated upon!

When we are not totally capable of controlling all the known variables, what hope do we have of controlling unknown variables?

Another problem is that what is unknown is always greater than what is known. For the human being the unknown has a wide scope, but the known is very limited. For instance, you know a given flower. You may even know that it is a rose, but you do not know why it is red or why it has these many petals, not more or fewer. When this is the extent of your knowledge, how are you going to control the hidden variables? Yet you want the results. Therefore, what are you going to do to control the hidden variables or even the known variables, since a mishap can always occur? As an agent, *kartṛ*, what can you do? You cannot do anything. Why is that? Only with reference to known variables, can you plan and do. You can take precautions. But how are you going to control the unknown variables? You cannot, because you do not know what they are. That is why they are called hidden variables. Therefore, in all cultures there is something called prayer, *prārthanā*. If you say that you do not require prayer, it means that you are not pragmatic, even though you tend to take yourself to be very pragmatic.

Our free will is not that 'free'

Prayer is an action; it comes from the *kartṛ*. This action is the only action where the *kartṛ* is functioning in full measure, coming under no pressure. It is the *kartṛ* who uses the will. In fact the will itself is called *kartṛ*. The experiencer, on the other hand, just experiences whatever there is. Will does not play any role while knowing, even while experiencing. The person is just cognitive. Whereas, the will is centred upon the *kartṛ*, the doer, who has the freedom to choose whether[2] to do an action, or do it differently—*kartum, akartum, anyathā vā kartuṁ śakyam*. The cognitive person does not have that freedom. If the object is a flower, I need to know it as flower. The freedom that is implied in the will is always subject to pressure, released by my likes and dislikes. So the free will is not totally free. The degree of freedom enjoyed by the will is determined by how much pressure is exerted upon the will.

One has this internal pressure to prove oneself. To whom should one prove oneself? Obviously, the self-image of the person is wanting, causing a pressure to prove one's adequacy. In the *Mahābhārata*, Karṇa was considered the most giving person. He was. The stories of what all he had given away are simply amazing. However on one occasion he said that, "I give to prove to the world that I am the most giving person." This was because he had an

---

[2] 'Whether or not' is a common expression but the correct usage is only 'whether' without being followed by 'or not'. Whether one likes this—grammatically this is right (Author).

image of himself that he did not accept. There was a fact about him that he knew which made him unacceptable in his own estimation. He was brought up by a *sūta*, a charioteer. He called himself *sūtaputra*, son of a charioteer, not knowing anything else about his divine, royal birth. He was a Kaunteya, born of Kuntī. She was given a boon that she could beget children by chanting *mantra*s of different Gods; one of them was the *sūrya-mantra*. She used it at the age of ten to see if the boon worked or not. Immediately there was a baby on her lap! Naturally, she panicked and put the baby in a box and floated it down the river with a prayer. The box with the baby was picked up by a charioteer. This first-born son of Kuntī, therefore, grew up as a *sūtaputra*. However, the feeling inside of him was unlike that of a *sūtaputra*. Karṇa was the greatest archer, even greater than Arjuna in some ways. He knew that he was the best, but still felt the need to prove himself due to inner pressure. He wanted to show that he was the best in various ways.

Following dharma helps us 'become' free

Giving is a *pūrta-karma*, one of the good actions, but if that action comes under the pressure of needing to prove oneself, the free will is not totally free. In every reaching out action there is free will involved because one need not do it. But when one does it, when one reaches out, it is out of free will, and that action can produce *puṇya*. Otherwise, being inhibited by pressure, the free will is less free; the result also is less.

The free will is totally absent in an impulsive action. If an animal kicks, it is instinctive but not when a human being does it. An action based on free will is a conscious action. A reaction, on the other hand, is mechanical, and it just happens. It happens to a human being who is supposed to choose and act. Where there is no deliberation, there is no freedom either. So you cannot say that such an action is an expression of free will. The action expressing free will is refraining from kicking and moving away from someone who kicks you! The latter is, in fact, spontaneous because it is the right thing to do. Therefore, you have to see how much freedom your will really enjoys. The more human you are when the will enjoys more freedom. This is where the possibility of your growth lies.

When we talk about *dharma*, we say, "Do your duty; do your *dharma*." These are statements addressed to our free will. Our task is to endow the will with all the freedom that it is capable of achieving. When we free the will from pressure, it is freer. That is why we say to our children, "Don't come under peer pressure." The fact is that we have the freedom to pick and choose. There is certain responsibility on the part of a human being to live intelligently, to know a few basic things. If we do not know them, we can always choose to learn; that is our responsibility.

One of the most important components in intelligent living is to seek help when one needs it. One has limited knowledge and limited power; one knows this. Therefore, one needs to seek help. One seeks help because one does not control all the variables, and one cannot determine the outcome. This is how human life is intelligently lived.

One has the responsibility of knowing things and seeking help, but still one comes under pressure. This pressure comes from one's own unconscious. Our *śāstra* very simply states that the pressure is caused by binding likes and dislikes, *rāga-dveṣa*. The *Bhagavad Gītā* refers[3] this pressure as *vega*, force, born of desire and anger. Anger itself is born of pain caused by unfulfilled desires. Then one comes under the spell of anger because of *vega*. The one who does not come under the influence of the pressure exerted by *kāma*—likes and dislikes—and anger, can gain self-knowledge. This is necessary not only for self-knowledge, but also to live a

---

[3] *śaknotīhaiva yaḥ soḍhuṁ prāk śarīravimokṣaṇāt*
kāmakrodhodbhavaṁ vegaṁ sa yuktaḥ sa sukhī naraḥ (5.23)
The one who is able to master the force born of anger and desire here (in this world) before release from the body is a *karma-yogin*. He (or she) indeed is a happy person.

life of certain degree of satisfaction, free from guilt; just to live one's life fairly, successfully as a human being.

Real success is not in terms of money, power, fame, and so on. The one who does not come under pressure is a *siddha*, a successful person. Therefore, how much freedom does a free-will-based action enjoys, is always in keeping with the degree of freedom the will has. Interestingly, the freer you become in terms of your free will, fewer the choices you have. Also, you do not fail to see the choices.

Life becomes simple because the things that are to be done become obvious; otherwise it becomes complex. To keep life simple is to hone the free will by releasing it from coming under pressure. If this is understood, then *pūrta-karma*s, altruistic activities, or 'charitable' *karma*s (I prefer to call them as 'reaching-out' actions; the word 'charity' connotes a patronising attitude) are generally considered free. If there is a patronising attitude, then the freedom is not that great, but, still, there is freedom because you choose to reach out. Naturally, action is totally free only when the agent of action is totally free. In fact, when you discover you are not a *kartṛ*, but an *akartṛ*, you are then totally free in your actions. Here, we are confining our discussion to the *kartṛ*, the doer that you are.

Prayer is the only 'completely free' action on the part of a kartṛ

What is the action in which this doer is free? I will say, 'prayer'. In reaching out actions when you see somebody in a situation requiring some help, due to empathy, you naturally pick up the pain of the person. Now the pain becomes yours. Then to get rid of that pain you reach out to the other, bringing redress to the person. For many people who are committed to earning and saving money, it is always hard to give. That is why *dānam,* giving, is a *puṇya-karma.* There is a lot of freedom in it. Easy things like smiling, anybody can do, but to really reach out, you have to do things that hurt you. The area that hurts you is the area where you have to grow. Giving to convincing causes is one of the great things that one can do. Still, there is a small degree of pressure caused by the situation therein.

The only area where an action does not come under any pressure is prayer. One may say that Draupadī did not pray until she came under pressure. She pleaded to all around her and everybody was helpless, and then she prayed to Lord Kṛṣṇa. Yes, she did come under pressure, but she could have committed suicide instead of praying. Prayer means recognising the presence of Īśvara. This is an entirely different type of action. Draupadī prayed to Śrī Kṛṣṇa and his grace made the *sari* lengthen. One can climb the wall, take to alcohol, go on a shopping spree, or end one's life; one need not pray. The ability to pray comes from the basic person who has either belief in or understanding of Īśvara, and also of the efficacy of prayer.

Primarily, prayer is for adṛṣṭa-phala, unseen result

When you use your free will and choose to do something meant to produce a desired result, then the pursuit is called *puruṣārtha*. What a person desires is called *puruṣārtha—puruṣaiḥ arthyate iti puruṣārthaḥ*. *Pravṛtti* is pursuit to achieve the *puruṣārtha*. The pursuit is generally either for *artha*, security, or for *kāma*, seeking certain pleasure and ego satisfaction. The pursuit of *artha* also gives you a sense of well-being. If money is pursued for security, it is *artha* because it gives certain sense of security. But if the pursuit is for ego-gratification like name, power, and so on, it is *kāma*. Both are meant for your well-being and so they are called *puruṣārtha*s. People are committed to these two *puruṣārtha*s. In attempting to achieve these *puruṣārtha*s, you face situations over which you have no control and you recognise them as hidden variables. When you do not control even the known variables, what control can you exercise over hidden variables? Therefore, we have another *puruṣārtha* called *dharma* (here *puṇya*). To avoid, to neutralise the hidden variables and make things happen we employ the means of prayer.

In every culture, which is connected to religion, there is certain form of prayer. The African tribes have a dance ritual for rains. It is a *kāyikaṁ karma*, a ritualistic prayer. While prayer is in all religions, what does it do is taught in our *śāstra*. Born of uninhibited free will, any form of prayer produces *adṛṣṭa* in different degrees, besides *dṛṣṭa-phala*, an immediately seen result, like freedom from frustration one gets. This is so because one has acted upon the desire to control the hidden variables, avoiding helplessness. The satisfaction that comes from praying is a visible result, *dṛṣṭa-phala*. There are other means to get satisfaction—one does not need prayer. Explaining away prayer, psychologically, is not at all correct. The means for *dṛṣṭa-phala* is called *laukika-karma*, like cooking and eating. If what is cooked is offered to the Lord and then consumed, it produces a different result. That is the result that we are talking about.

Every form of prayer, whether it is a highly sophisticated prayer like an elaborate Vedic ritual, *yāga*, or the simple prayer of a tribal person, is meant for *adṛṣṭa*, a result that is not seen now. This *adṛṣṭa* is not discussed much in other traditions except in Buddhism, which is also part of our own *dharma*. The *adṛṣṭa* is what I call the law of *karma*, and it does not include the known means and ends. When I talk about the law of *karma,* I mean only *adṛṣṭa.* When I have a choice, the choice to employ certain means for an end, whether *artha* or *kāma,* that choice can be wrong or right. Whenever there is choice, there can be an error. If there is a switch, for instance, I can flip it up or down and get a different result. I should know which action produces what result. When I have a choice of means to achieve *puruṣārtha*s, the chosen means can either conform to or transgress *dharma.*

I can go against *dharma* due to pressure, born of confused values of *puruṣārtha*s. Every human being is clear as to what every other living being should do to him or her: "The whole world should behave properly towards me; even the planetary Gods should be my benefactors by aligning themselves properly for me. Nobody should cheat me, hurt me, sue me or take advantage of me. Everybody should be compassionate, giving, sharing, and nice." Even a mafia don expects all his capos to tell him the truth.

I also know that others expect the same from me and therefore I cannot plead ignorance with respect to my expectations of others' behaviour towards me, and also I cannot plead ignorance of what others expect of me. Both are very clear to me. Thus, we already have a common basis for interaction. God does not mandate this at a given time in human history.

If every individual has to be taught these values, *dharma*, then right and wrong could never be universal. Not all would be fortunate enough to be taught. But, that is not the case. If you ask any human being on this earth whether he or she wants to get hurt, you will get the same response, 'No.' Nobody wants to be hurt and nobody wants to be cheated. This is a common order. This is a manifestation, a critical manifestation, of the Lord, Īśvara, who is all-knowledge.

The world is a manifestation of Īśvara

When you see a watch, you know that it was put together by an intelligent being. When you look at your body, senses, etc., you should know that they are all intelligently put together. You presuppose certain knowledge behind that, and that knowledge has to rest in a conscious being. Therefore, you appreciate the all-knowledge Īśvara who is manifest as the cause of all that is known and unknown to you. No scientist would be against this statement. But they are up against the concept of a God who is in a place called heaven, which needs to be in space and time. The scientist, having figured out the fact that space and time come together along with this world, naturally, is not going to accept a God who has a location in space and time.

The probability for this universe not to exist is much greater than the probability for it to be here.

The motion, the progression to form the universe from sub-atomic particles, seem to stem from the knowledge of what is going to be. Scientists do appreciate that mere particles cannot move like that. Our eyes are particles, no doubt; but how do they assemble themselves to form eyes? A liver? They are intelligent, not dumb. We also say that they are intelligent. In fact we say they are not separate from the intelligence. There is an intelligent being, and the material for the universe is not separate from this intelligent being. What we call the world, *jagat*, is but a manifestation of this being; it is not really a creation. We would call it a 'creation' only from the standpoint of knowledge and methodical progression. From the standpoint of the material that is not separate from Īśvara, it is a manifestation. If that is so, all that is manifest is that being, Īśvara. *Dharma* is also Īśvara because it is there; we uniformly sense it by our common sense.

Conforming to dharma is being in harmony with Īśvara

Dharma is not concocted by some given minds. We all commonly sense *dharma*, and so it is universal. When we commonly sense something, what is sensed is already there. I can commit a mistake in what I sense, and you can commit a mistake in what you sense, but if we all sense it, universally, correctly, then that thing exists. Nobody has seen gravitational force, it is not visible. Yet we all know it exists, including every monkey. When it jumps from one branch to another, it makes sure that its leap is just adequate to reach its target; and it does not need to learn from anyone. Even a baby monkey knows to hold on to its mother. That means we all commonly sense gravitational force. Similarly, we all sense *dharma*. It is required for the human being.

As a human being I have to make choices. When I make a choice and if I conform to the common norm, it does not hurt anybody. When I conform to the norm, I conform to Īśvara. The *jīva*, the ego, which is a spin-off from Īśvara for the time being, tries to subserve *dharma*, Īśvara; one surrenders to Īśvara. In other words, the *jīva* is a *bhakta*, a devotee. One way of looking at this is that Īśvara becomes the ruler, and the *jīva* becomes a *bhṛtya*, the one who serves Īśvara. This is called, 'the maxim of the master and servant, *swāmi-bhṛtya-nyāya*.' The *Vaiṣṇava* saints have brought out this idea very well in their hymns—I am the *bhṛtya*, devotee, and you are the *swāmi*, the Lord who is manifest in the form of *dharma*. When I conform to *dharma*, then I do not get estranged from Īśvara.

The popular saying, 'thy will be done,' would mean that Īśvara's will which is *dharma* will be done. Conformity to *dharma* is being in harmony with Īśvara, being imbued with the presence of Īśvara.

Therefore, the ego of one who transgresses *dharma* is under the pressure of desire. Īśvara sustains even this ego; the psychological order also being Īśvara. This is what is meant when one is asked to surrender one's ego. Going against *dharma,* is *adharma.* Every animal, including a carnivorous, is dharmic because animals are programmed; they have no choice. Whereas a human being is privileged with the faculty of choice and can use it to be dharmic or abuse it to be adharmic. Therefore, one's growth lies in allowing Īśvara to rule one's life through adherence to *dharma;* more the *dharma,* more Īśvara there is in one's life because the Lord is manifest as *dharma.*

Why should anybody be given to *adharma*? It is because of the inner pressure. A person is given to crime because of this pressure, and this pressure is much greater in some people due to their background. The habitual offenders are those who are not able to find a way to manage this pressure. To label them is not helpful to anyone. No person is a born-criminal; he is made into a person given to crime. There is no evil. In Sanskrit, we do not have a word for evil. There is *dharma-adharma,* and *puṇya-pāpa,* but no concept of evil. God is not 'either or'— "Either you follow me, or I will send you to hell."

Now a crime also is *karma;* it produces a result. Since there is an element of free will, the action is going to attract an undesirable result, *adṛṣṭa-pāpa.*

When you conform to *dharma* and reach out, or you perform an act of prayer, the result is *puṇya*. When you go against *dharma,* you may be able to get away from the man-made laws, but you have to pay for it later, *pāpa,* the result being there. So too, *puṇya* results in desirable situations, now or later. This is the law of *karma*.

Prayer produces puṇya

Dharma is on one side of the coin and *karma* is on the other side, both are manifestations of Īśvara. When I abuse my free will, and go against *dharma,* naturally, I have to pay for it; I am responsible for my actions. While *pāpa* always translates itself into an unpleasant situation, *puṇya* fructifies into a pleasant situation.

Sometimes, a person would abuse his or her free will causing an unpleasant situation for me. Even though that person has to pay for it still, now or later, I am affected. That is why *dharma* has to be lived by all; only then does it work. A human life is to be lived in a responsible way. If one person is following *dharma,* while everyone else is following *adharma,* it will not work. One cannot live one's life that way. That is a problem, and to solve it we require an *avatāra*.

Dharma or *karma* is not an ordinary topic; it is very complex. "…the course of *karma* cannot be fathomed;

gahanā karmaṇo gatiḥ."[4] It is enough for you to understand that you are responsible for your actions, and that these actions produce two kinds of results, *dṛṣṭa* and *adṛṣṭa,* which can be *puṇya* or *pāpa*. There are no words in English for *puṇya* and *pāpa*. When a mosquito bites you, we can say that you exhaust some *pāpa* and gain a little bit of *puṇya*. A little bit of *pāpa* going in the bite is understandable. Where is *puṇya*? Every biting mosquito is a pregnant mosquito, and by giving blood to a pregnant woman who needs a bloodmeal, you are gaining *puṇya*! When unavoidable or unpleasant situations come, the wisemen, *paṇḍitas*, do not worry because some *pāpa* is exhausted. When you kill the mosquito you gain a little *pāpa,* and that can be neutralised by reaching out *karmas* or performing a ritual or a prayer.

We have to control many hidden variables caused by *pāpa*. So it is better that we pile up the *puṇya,* grace, to neutralise or minimise the hidden variables that cause unpleasant situations. That is why we pray all the time, while cooking, before eating, while entering the newly-built house, while starting the car first time in the day, before starting any construction and so on. Prayers are actions and therefore they have results.

The definition of *karma* is that which is centred on an agent, *kartṛ-tantra*. An action born of will is

---

[4] *Bhagavad Gītā* 4-17

karma, and so only the one who is endowed with will can perform *karma*. There is a definition of *karma*—*calanātmakaṁ karma*, meaning, that which implies motion or change is *karma*. If that is so, then anything that moves is doing *karma*; the air is doing *karma*, water is doing *karma*, and the earth is doing *karma*. Even though we accept that certain forces initiate the motion, we do not really consider this *karma*. *Karma* has to come from the will of a person.

On this planet, the human being has the highest degree of free will. Where there is free will, *karma* is possible. Therefore, the definition of *karma* is *kartṛ-tantram*, centred on the *kartṛ*. So, we have to say *calanātmakam api karma kartṛ-tantram*, even though there is motion in *karma*, the definition implies 'centred on *kartṛ*'. This kind of *karma* attracts *puṇya* and *pāpa*. That there is *puṇya* and *pāpa* for *karma* is known through the means of knowledge that is other than perception, inference and so on.

Śāstra reveals the existence of adṛṣṭa-phala

No knowledge occurs without a *pramāṇa*, a means of knowing, and each *pramāṇa* is independent and self-validating. What can be known by one means of knowledge, at a given time and place, cannot be known by another means of knowledge. You may infer that there is fire at this time and place because you can see the smoke, but the fire is available for direct perception at a different time and place. That is why time and place are very important because you can only infer what can be inferred. For any knowledge, you require an appropriate means of knowledge. It becomes clear that what has to be seen in terms of eyesight cannot be gained by any other means of knowledge. To see colour, you have to use your eyes. The form can be discerned through the sense of touch, but only your eyes can see colour. For what can be heard, you have to use only your ears, and not your eyes. In other words, an appropriate means of knowledge needs to be employed to gain knowledge of a given object. *Puṇya* is not going to be seen by you, much less *pāpa*. Once the *karma* is performed and its immediate result is received, nothing is left that can become the basis for making the inference that there is *puṇya* or *pāpa*. Therefore, *śabda*, the Veda, is the means of knowledge for *puṇya* and *pāpa*.

Human life is a mixture of puṇya and pāpa

The *śāstra* tells me that these two types of *karmaphala*, *puṇya* and *pāpa*, further result in pleasant and unpleasant experiences. That there is *puṇya* and *pāpa* is known only through the means of knowledge called *śabda*, the words of the Veda. Having said that, I can say that it is not totally against my experience, in that, what is revealed by the Veda is confirmed by my own experience. Why should a person, who had been very careful in investing all his life, suddenly pull out money from his money manager and invest it in high-tech stocks? Astrologers will say that the period of Saturn, *śani-daśā*, has begun. He has to lose and he loses. Saturn is only an indicator in the astrological model to interpret his own *karma*.

One's experience makes one appreciate the presence of something that places one in the right place at the right time, or in the right place at the wrong time. Every road accident occurs when two vehicles are necessitated to occupy the same place at the same time. The laws of physics do allow this—only in both the vehicles hitting each other. In fact, accidents are only incidents, the causes of which are not yet known. Once the traffic police investigate and come to know the cause of the accident reducing it to an incident, one is punished and the other goes free. Does one punish the person for the accident or the incident? Only an ascertained fact can satisfy the requirements for punishment. Otherwise, how the court is going to punish anybody?

Why should you be at the right place but at the wrong time? It reveals something over which you have no control. That is what I call the hidden variable. You do not have total control over all this. This is human experience of even the primitive man when he went hunting for food. He hunts the whole day and returns to the cave with a single squirrel. Another day he catches a deer within 15 minutes of leaving his cave! I am sure he understood the difference between diffcult and easy day. To convey this human experience, a word must be there in every dialect to describe luck. Even when there is no dialect, one has to communicate the experience by some sign language. What is it that accounts for this common human experience? Astrologers try to figure out whether there is a recognisable pattern, a pattern that is born with you with the help of something that can be discerned.

You miss the bus sometimes, and sometimes you get the bus. Some people get the bus more often than not. Some others miss it more often than not. In certain periods of time you get the bus more often than not. In another period of time, you find that you keep missing the bus. Thus, you find a mixture of pleasant and unpleasant experiences that you cannot account for; you understand *śāstra*'s words such as *puṇya* and *pāpa* are hidden variables.

Environment and parentage contribute to the lot of a person. A child born in America to Indian parents is definitely not going to be the same as the one born in India at the same time. It is tough for Indian children to grow up in America because the child is wondering why he or she is different from all others who are white. One's own *puṇya* and *pāpa* account for one's time, place, parentage and other situations. The *karma* of a human being is a mixture, *miśrātmakaṁ karma*. If one has predominantly *puṇya* one becomes a *devatā*, a celestial, and if one has predominantly *pāpa*, one will be born in lower *yoni*s, wombs. The mixture results in a human being.

Without *puṇya* and *pāpa*, how one is going to explain good luck and bad luck? Nothing much is explained when one simply says one is lucky or unlucky. One only points out a hidden variable which confirms the point that there is such a thing as *adṛṣṭa*. This *adṛṣṭa*, consisting of *puṇya* and *papa*, was gathered by free will. A water buffalo is not going to attract any *puṇya* or *pāpa* because it has no free will; there is no *karma* for it; there is only experience, *anubhava*. Animals are only experiencers, and not willful agents. They experience their *prārabdha* which also consists of *puṇya-pāpa*. For instance, there is a lucky dog which always travels in a car, eats good food, etc., while a street dog is not as lucky. However, the lucky dog does not think that it is lucky. That is the privilege of a human being.

Neither the *devatā*s nor the animals can attract any *puṇya-pāpa* because they have no free will; they are only *bhoktṛ*s. Their life can be likened to your going on a holiday where you spend only your money. You keep spending from the money you have which is limited, accumulated from a finite amount of *karma*.

The same is true of a human being who goes to heaven. A finite quantity of *puṇya* will keep you in heaven for a finite period of time; you then come back when your *puṇya* is exhausted. To decide whether a person is capable of earning *puṇya* or *pāpa*, the only criterion is free will. The *puṇya* and *pāpa* were gathered because of the free will the *jīva* had in many births.

In this birth also you have free will and you will continue to gather *puṇya-pāpa*. The free will is going to run concurrently with situations created by the *prārabdha-karma*. By a ritual of prayer, *your puṇya* can be enhanced and *your pāpa* can be neutralised. By prayer, what comes to your neck may only take away your hat, as it happened to Arjuna when Karṇa released the *nāgāstra*, the serpent missile. This is very nicely illustrated by a story.

Two urchins were walking from one village to another. On the way they came across a temple of Lord Gaṇeśa. In our culture you cannot pass a temple without offering *namaskāra*. One boy went into the temple, while the other did not because he did not have a value for temple worship. As he was walking about slowly for his friend to catch him up, he found a gold coin. The boy who went into the temple was stung by a scorpion on his right toe, when he was coming out. As he lay crying from the painful, burning sensation, the other boy taunted him, "You get only a scorpion sting for your temple visit, see, what I have found." Saying this he showed the shining gold coin. Wreathing in burning pain the other boy became sad over this unassimilable divine justice.

Just then a *mahātmā* passing that way happened to see these boys; one of them was crying in pain. On enquiry he found that the boy was stung by a scorpion for which the *mahātmā* gave some medicines. Then the boy asked him, "Swamiji, we both are friends, going to the next village. On the way, I went to the temple to have *darsan* and on my way back I got this scorpion sting. My friend said that he did not believe in temple visit and he picked up a gold coin. If there is any divine justice, I should get the gold coin. Is there any explanation?"

The *mahātmā* was an expert astrologer. He got from them certain facts, their birthdate, time and place, and prepared their natal charts. Studying them he told each one of them his entire past accurately and said further that one was to meet with a severe accident and escaped from it with a scorpion bite. Whereas, the other was to have a jackpot for which he was having a lottery ticket, but had to settle for a coin because of his act of criticising temple worship; that reduced his *puṇya*.

We need to know the ways of *karma*, it is too complex for us to comprehend, but we know a good *karma* done with free will is bound to produce *puṇya*.

If someone is progressing or being lucky, it is due to *karma* done previously, *pūrva-karma*. Therefore, we have to understand that the *prārabdha-karma* that has brought us into being is being unfolded every day. This mixture of *puṇya-pāpa* keeps unfolding unexpectedly everyday, every hour, and every minute of our life. We plan so many things, but things do not always go the way we want. Some days, something else works along with our *puruṣārtha*, and some other days it does not; something works against it. Therefore what do we do? We pray. We have got to pray to neutralise the *pāpa* and enhance the *puṇya*.

Ritualistic Prayer

Prayer is *karma*, an action. It is three-fold: *kāyika*, *vācika*, and *mānasa*, and is based upon the means that we employ. *Kāyikaṁ karma* is a ritualistic act in which the limbs are employed, *vācikaṁ karma* is oral prayer such as recitation, chanting, and singing. Speech, *vāk*, is also used in *kāyikaṁ karma*, and the mind is used in both *kāyikaṁ* and *vācikaṁ karma*. Then we have a third type of *karma*, which is purely mental, *mānasaṁ karma*.

Śrauta-karma

We need to daily perform these three-fold *karma*. The *śāstra* enjoins *nitya-karma*, daily to-be-done *karma*, to neutralise the accumulated *pāpa*, also called *durita*, and enhance your *puṇya*.

Suppose I have performed an action which I know I should not have done, I can do a *karma* called *prāyaścitta-karma*, for atonement. There are various forms of *prāyaścitta*, each meant to neutralise the result of a given wrong action. This type of *karma* includes fire-rituals, pilgrimage, *dānam*-giving, fasting, and so on.

There are other *karma*s that are to be performed on occasions, like on the day of solar and lunar eclipse, death anniversary of parents, one's sixtieth birthday and so on. These *karma*s also enhance one's *puṇya* and neutralise one's *pāpa*.

We also have *kāmya-karma*. This is a *karma* or ritual performed for a particular desired result. If we want rain, for instance, there is a particular *karma* for that. Then there is a ritual called *putrakāmeṣṭi* for the birth of a child. There is also a ritual for gaining entry into *svarga*. All these are *kāmya-karma*s, done for achieving ends that fall under the category of either *artha* or *kāma*.

Karma-yoga is based upon these *karma*s. If most of these *karma*s are done for the purification of oneself with a change of attitude, then it is *karma-yoga*. These are all *śrauta karma*s. A *śrauta karma* is that which is revealed by the *śruti*—*śruti-vihita-karma śrautam*.

Smārta-karma

There is another category of *karma* called *smārta-karma*, a *karma* enjoined by the *smṛti*, *smṛti-vihita-karma smārtam*. *Smṛti* is another body of literature, which is based upon the *śruti*, written by individuals who understood the nuances of *śruti*. It supports the *śruti*, but never goes against the *śruti*. On the other hand, *śruti* was not composed, but received by sages. It is revelation. *Śruti-mantra*s are used in some of the more sophisticated *smārta-karma*s. These are all called *kāyikaṁ karma* or ritualistic prayers.

Ritualistic prayer produces the maximum puṇya

Kāyikaṁ karma, ritualistic prayer, involves materials and an altar entailing physical action. *Mantra*s are involved, the speech, *vāk,* is used, and the mind, of course, is necessary for the successful execution of any *karma*. Since all the *karaṇa*s, the mind, speech, and the physical limbs, are involved, on the basis of the general rule, *adhikasya adhikaṁ phalam*, this *karma* is the most efficacious in producing *puṇya*. This rule, *nyāya,* means, 'more the effort, more is the result.' In terms of *karaṇa*, effort, expenditure, number of people and materials, oral and mental prayers cannot come anyway near a physical ritual's efficacy in producing *puṇya*.

Many religions have lost ritual worship because they do not worship forms. Still, they need some rituals, and have, therefore, created altars and liturgy to offer prayer and perform some rituals accompanied by language, a physical posture, hand gestures, direction, pilgrimage, taboos and musts. All these are not forms? In fact, there are rites performed by the priests.

A ritual is looked upon as one action in which you are complete as a person with free will. The whole person is involved, with the Lord as the altar, and the world is involved in the form of the materials used.

For gaining maximum *puṇya,* there is no substitute for a ritual. Even though oral worship has its own result, it is always less than that of ritualistic worship. All the *karma*s that we have mentioned here, *prāyaścitta, nitya, naimittika,* and *kāmya,* are *kāyikaṁ karma.* All of them are prayers which produce *adṛṣṭa,* the presence of which is revealed by human experience. Otherwise, you would have to settle for the concept of luck and chance, leaving you helpless.

Altars

In a fire ritual, a religiously lighted fire is the altar in which oblations are offered not only to *agni-devatā,* deity of fire, but also to different *devatā*s; it is all Īśvara viewed from standpoints.

You can also create an altar by invoking a particular deity in a *kalaśa,* a pot of water, in a lamp, or in a traditional form which is either a picture or icon to offer your worship. The worship has certain rules. You need not follow all the rules, and can still offer worship. At home, you have a *pūjā* room, may be in a corner, where you offer a simple *pūjā* every day. Without a *pūjā* room, a house is not a home!

There are very elaborate rituals involving as many as 300 priests, or simple *karma*s involving one or no priests. The *agnihotra,* for instance, is done by an individual, and in this ritual, only two oblations are offered—once in the morning and again in the evening. The *vājapeya-yajña* is the ritual one does after performing a series of rituals which include *darśa-pūrṇamāsa* and *soma-yāga*. So, the *adhikāra* for *vājapeya* is only for the one who has completed the other required rituals. This is called *adhikṛtasya adhikāraḥ*. The one who has done *vājapeya* is called a *vājapeyī*. Similarly, the one who has performed the *soma-yāga* is a *somayājī*, and the one who performs the *agnihotra* is an *agnihotrī*.

Daily *sandhyā-vandana* is a *kāyikaṁ karma*, done with oblations of water, Vedic chanting and *gāyatri-mantra* chanting, three times a day. Those who are initiated into *gāyatrī* do this *karma*. *Samidādhāna* is a fire ritual performed by the *gāyatrī* initiated students, bachelors, praying for brilliance, health and spiritual strength. *Surya-namaskāra*, is also a *kāyikaṁ karma*; a prayer exercise done daily.

Oral Prayer

Oral prayer, *vācikaṁ karma*, is common to every religion. Being oral, it consists of hymns, verses, prose and songs in praise of the Lord. These are called in Sanskrit, *sūkta, śloka, gadya,* and *gītam* respectively. A *sūkta* is from any of the Vedas as even *mantras*. *Gāyatrī* is one such *mantra*. Any Vedic *mantra* has its *svaras* and notations which we have to chant only with those *svaras*. The Vedic hymns are also to be chanted with *svaras* for which one has to undergo training. If one has no training, one can listen to a tape daily; it is as good as chanting if one listens attentively with a book in hand. Ere long one will pick up the mode of chanting.

When you chant a *sūkta* with some understanding of the meaning of the words, you are really praying to the Lord through the Vedic hymn. On the other hand, the verses of the *Bhagavad Gītā* have no *svaras*, they are to be recited with some repetitive musical notes. *Gītam* which is also called *kirtana* is to be sung in a praticular melody whose entire range is brought out. The lyric and music have the capacity to bring about certain elevation and absorption. Therefore, you require music in *gītam*.

All names are Īśvara's names

All words are the Lord's names because everything is a manifestation of Īśvara. While every word is his name, we do have significant names like Hari, Hara and so on. Why? The word, 'tree' means only tree; it does not mean the sun, the moon, or the earth. However, special words like Hari, Hara, Śiva and so on include every form, each name having its own special connotation.

A *nāma,* name, has a *nāmin,* an object to reveal. Without an object there is no *nāma*. There is a relationship between a name and its object, *nāma-nāmi-sambandha,* as between a word and its meaning, *vāg-artha-sambandha*. When I show you a rose, you recognise it and the word 'rose' pops up in your mind. Since you have memory, you can think of a lake while you are travelling through a desert. The object need not be objectified by the senses. Once you know the meaning of the word, the object, you cannot say the word without thinking of its meaning.

The *sambandha* between the *vāk* and its *artha* is established by repeated exposure and education. Once you have that connection, then the name and its corresponding object are inseparable. Kālidāsa praises the Lord in this way.

वागर्थाविव सम्पृक्तौ वागर्थप्रतिपत्तये ।
जगतः पितरौ वन्दे पार्वतीपरमेश्वरौ ॥

vāg-arthāviva sampṛktau vāg-artha-pratipattaye,
jagataḥ pitarau vande pārvatī-parameśvarau.

> I worship Pārvatī and Parameśvara, the parents of the world, who are inseparable, like a word and its meaning, in order to understand words and their meanings.

The Lord Parameśvara and his power, the *māyā-śakti* symbolised by Goddess Pārvatī, are inseparable. Without Īśvarī, there is no Īśvara; and there is no Īśvarī without Īśvara either. They are together like a word and its meaning. What an example! Kālidāsa begins his *kāvya, Raghuvaṁśa,* with this striking prayer: "I am going to write the glories of the king Raghu and all others in Śrī Rāma's lineage. All of them were illustrious kings. What is the *prabhāva,* the glory of this lineage, and what is my mind? It is too small, inadequate (to capture all the glories of these kings). Therefore, oh Lord, please give me the power of seeing the nuances of words, *vāg-artha-pratipattaye.*" All the nuances of all words need to strike him because Kālidāsa is going to capture and present, in the form of poems, the great kings and their amazing qualities and deeds.

You can invoke Īśvara in a particular name

Among the many special names and forms of the Lord, you can have a name and form for the three-fold prayer. This is called *iṣṭa-devatā,* chosen form and name of Īśvara. What does the word 'Rāma' mean to you? The Lord. Kṛṣṇa? The Lord. Nārāyaṇa?

The Lord. Śiva? The Lord. Gaṇeśa? The Lord. Every word is the Lord. Suppose I ask you, "Think of the Lord." Who comes to your mind? "Rāma." That is your *iṣṭa-devatā*. When Īśvara is understood as one who is all, you can choose any one special name and form to invoke the Lord and offer the prayers. The attitude of generations of people, towards words like Rāma and so on, have created an inseparable meaning along with an appropriate *bhāvanā*, attitude. You invoke Īśvara by a particular name and form.

Let us look at the name Hari in the '*hare rāma hare kṛṣṇa*' *kīrtana*. The one who takes away all *pāpa* is Hari, *harati pāpāni iti hariḥ*. You are relating to Lord as a devotee, a *bhakta*. The words, Hari or Rāma or Kṛṣṇa, invoke the devotee, who is the basic individual.

You are son-brother-father; daughter-sister-mother and so on, but who are you? You are a simple conscious being who assumes these various roles. This being, without playing any role, is related to whom? The basic individual is related to the total, *samaṣṭi*. In the total manifestation, you are an individual with one body-mind-sense complex. This is a single conscious being, but like a tree in the forest. The forest-ness pervades the tree, but the tree is not the forest.

The individual body-mind-sense complex is pervaded by Īśvara, but with reference to that single body-mind-sense complex, one is a *jīva*. That *jīva* is a simple conscious being, and the simple conscious being is related to the total, Īśvara.

A God who has a location in a theology, cannot be the creation itself. He can only be like a king ruling the universe. Such a God becomes time-bound and therefore limited. A religious pursuit becomes meaningful only when Īśvara is total. He cannot be vengeful. When you say *samaṣṭi* it means that the total manifestation is Īśvara. You are included in that, yet related to Īśvara. When you use a means to invoke that Īśvara, who includes everything, then, related to that Īśvara, you are a devotee. When you think of your daughter, the parent in you is invoked. When you think of Īśvara, the basic person in you is invoked. The basic person is ever related to Īśvara. That is why that relationship does not vary. It is always the same. Your grandfather related to Īśvara in the same way, individual to total. Your father related to Īśvara in the same way, individual to total. You relate to Īśvara in the same way, individual to total. On the other hand, whereas, your grandfather related to your father, as a father, you relate to your father as son. The son becomes father, and thus, all other relationships are variable. The relationship to Īśvara, however, is an invariable relationship; it is between an individual and the total. This devotee pervades and sustains every role. While the role is this person, the person is not the role. The one who has this knowledge is a devotee, *bhakta*. That devotee is invoked when you say, '*hare rāma hare rāma rāma rāma hare hare*.'

The *adṛṣṭa-phala* is less for oral prayer than for *kāyikaṁ karma*, but the *dṛṣṭa-phala* is greater. The devotee is invoked and it cheers you up. This is called *laya*. In mental prayer, the *dṛṣṭa-phala* is even greater.

Mental Prayer

Meditation is mental activity focused on Īśvara

In *mānasaṁ karma* there is directed mental activity, *mānasa-vyāpāra*. One can do an elaborate ritual mentally, creating an altar, offering flowers and so on. There are verses describing in detail this mental worship, *mānasa-pūjā* and one can combine these forms. For example once can do a simple ritual and then an elaborate *pūjā* mentally. This combination of *kāyika-karma* and *mānasa-karma* is *jñāna-karma-samuccaya*. *Jñāna* here is meditation which is defined as *saguṇa-brahma-viṣaya-mānasa-vyāpāraḥ*.

Guṇa means attribute. With the prefix *sa* it means with attributes. Brahman is *satyaṁ jñānam anantam*. It is attribute-free, *nirguṇa*, limitless consciousness, which is the truth of everything and is the nature of the self, *ātman*. With *māyā-śakti* it becomes Īśvara, and once it is Īśvara, it is *saguṇa*. The word, 'Brahman' can mean *saguṇa* and *nirguṇa*. *Saguṇaṁ brahma* is Bhagavān, the one who has *bhaga*, limitless *guṇa*s like overlordship-*aiśvarya*, knowledge-*jñāna*, and so on. Everybody is *saguṇa* inasmuch as everyone has his or her own *guṇa*s. Even space has its own *guṇa*. Everything is a manifestation of *saguṇaṁ brahma*. Therefore, the manifest form will be *saguṇa*. The unmanifest is also *saguṇa*. *Sattva*, *rajas* and *tamas* are all there in the unmanifest condition, like even a seed in which the tree is not seen but it has all the *guṇa*s of the tree latent in it.

Saguṇaṁ brahma becomes the *viṣaya,* the object for the mental activity. Suppose I say, "Think." You will ask me, "Think of what?" That 'what' is the object, the *viṣaya,* of your thought. When I say that *dhyāna* is *saguṇa-brahma-viṣayam,* it will not mean only meditation but also oral prayer and ritual prayer as well, because they are all *saguṇa-brahma-viṣayam*.

If you define without adding *saguṇa-brahma,* obviously it will mean that any form of mental activity is meditation. Even worry is mental activity. Meditation is not any mental activity, nor is it emptying the mind of thoughts. *Vyāpāra* is activity. *Mānasa-vyāpāra* is mental activity. For this activity, the Lord is the object in meditation. Therefore in meditation you have to highlight the connection between yourself and the Lord through mental prayer whether with an altar-form or a chant-repetition (*japa*).

It is interesting to note that the word,'meditation' is used in English language in different connotations, all having a common meaning of mental action. Look at the meaning in these expressions: 'pre-meditated murder,' 'a decision after meditation,' and so on. So, the word 'meditation has to be qualified by *saguṇa-brahma-viṣaya*. Every word in the definition '*saguṇa-brahma-viṣaya*' has to be there to mean meditation.

To arrive at the meditator, you need to be objective. The more objective you are, the more relaxed you are. To meditate you follow a few steps such as posture, letting go concerns and agenda for others, paying attention to your breathing and watching your mind for a few seconds. Some people incorrectly present one of these steps as meditation. Even though it will help you relax and gain a degree of quietude, it is not the deliberate mental activity focused on the Lord, *saguṇa-brahma-viṣaya*. So you can visualise an altar and do an elaborate mental *pūjā*. In fact, the verses in *Śiva-mānasa-pūjā*[5] show the steps for doing *mānasa-pūjā*.

You offer a seat, *āsana*, as you do when a revered guest comes to your house. *Pādya*, washing the feet, *arghya*, offering water for washing the hands, *snāna*-bath, then clothes-*vastra*, ornaments-*ābharaṇa*, and flowers-*puṣpa*, these are all offered in a *pūjā*. Further, sandal paste-*candana*, kumkum-vermillion,[6] incense-*dhūpa*, showing light-*dīpa*, food-*naivedya*, are offered. The *āsana* offered is inlaid with precious stones, and

---

5 Refer the section '*mantras* and *stotras*'.

6 Red colour used by Hindus as a religious mark on their foreheads.

the food offered is elaborate. You need to see any given object in all its dimensions. In this act of worship the devotion grows and the devotee becomes real. Alienation from Īśvara disappears in time. The secondary result, *avāntara-phala*, is this that it enhances the capacity to hold an object in your mind for a length of time, in deep absorption. Depth and creativity would be lasting.

When the altar is there in your mind, the flowers are gone. When you offer the flowers, the altar is gone. This is common. But in this meditation, you learn to hold both at the same time. You can chant the Vedic hymns with *svaras*; your power to hold a topic, to look at it from all sides becomes effortless in time. All these capacities you learn in the process of doing meditation in the form of mental *pūjā*. In this *pūjā* you can see the meaning of the definition of *dhyāna*, meditation, as *saguṇa-brahma-viṣayamānasa-vyāpāra*.

Japa

The other form of meditation is *japa*, repetition of a meaningful chant connecting you to the Lord. This chant can be the one you are initiated in, or the one just chosen by you with a prayer, among the popular *mantras* like *'oṁ namaḥ śivāya' 'oṁ namo nārāyaṇāya' 'hare rāma…'* and so on. You need to stick to the same *mantra* unless you are given a new *mantra* by a competent person. The mental chanting has to be purely mental; no voice or breath gets associated. Real mental chanting itself rewards you with absorption (*savikalpa-samādhi*). This is *dṛṣṭa-phalam.*

Prāṇāyāma, while chanting *oṁ bhūḥ, oṁ bhuvaḥ,* etc., is for physical as well as inner cleansing, *śuddhi.* Meditation is an important part of worship in the Vedic culture and many people practice this in their daily lives. Mental chanting of *gāyatrī-mantra* is the most popular meditation. This *japa*-meditation has one more *dṛṣṭa-phalam.* No human being can predict what would be his or her next thought. The mind follows certain logic and has the capacity to move from one object to another through some form of connection, because everything is connected. You can move from the thought of a mountain to the thought of Lord Śiva. "This picture of mountain is very nice. I should visit the Himalayas. I think I should go to Kailāsa, the abode of Lord Śiva." Thus, one object can lead you to think of another. This is not a matter for complaint, but this is how the human mind operates. Both rhyme and logic can take the human mind to a world of fantasy. In the process you can become sad, depressed. All that you need is to think in a certain way. You have certain selective memory of events in your life that leads you to call yourself a failure. Even if you have had many successes, you do not always remember them, but you remember your failures leading to sadness.

Somebody has to keep telling you all the time that you are okay because the other side of you is very powerful. It is sometimes fraught with guilt and hurt; therefore it is more powerful. However, you have to think about that in order to become sad; otherwise you would not be sad. That is why you are not sad in sleep! There is no sadness, jealousy, or hatred without your thinking about it in certain patterns. Certainly you have no commitment to sadness. Then why do you think in this way? It is because you do not have any say over the ways of your mind.

Japa helps train our mind

To gain this 'say,' you need to have a chosen occupation so that any deviation from that can be discerned. In *japa*, the same chant is repeated. So you know what should be the next thought. Any thought other than the chosen chant can provide an occasion to bring the mind back to chanting. That is the practice of meditation.

In normal thinking, there is always connection; one thing leads to another, which leads to another, and so on. Unless you have a chosen point of reference like *japa*, there is no distraction. A chicory plant is a weed when you are trying to grow grass; on the other hand, the grass is a weed when you are trying to grow chicory. There is no such thing as a weed.

There are only plants. So any thought, however important it is, becomes a distraction when we are committed to *japa*. Each chant ends and the new one is the same. In the interval there is link in the form of any lingering contact. Therefore, the interval between chants is important.

I am conscious of the interval between chants. The interval and the one who is conscious are one and the same, object being not there, there is no subject-object relationship. "I am in the form of chant, I am in the form of interval." Initially, being conscious of the interval helps me avoid distraction. Even if there is one, I can bring myself back to chanting. No doubt there is a catch here. The one who has to bring the mind back is the one who has gone with the distracting thought. So here, I have to use the power of auto-suggestion. I have to suggest to myself that, "I will bring the mind back whenever it moves away." I have to make this suggestion in so many words before I begin chanting. This auto-suggestion comes to my help whenever there is distraction, making me aware of the distraction. Never make a suggestion saying, "I will chant without any distraction." This suggestion is against the nature of the mind; it is not based on reality. The mind will move away; instead guilt and frustration would be the result of meditation. Lord Kṛṣṇa says all this in the sixth chapter of the *Gītā* in the verse[7]: '*yato yato niścarati...*' Here *abhyāsa*, regular practice, is the means to gain a say over the ways of the mind. The level of my interaction with the world would be from where compassion reigns supreme. This is self-mastery without which I become my own enemy.[8] On the other hand I become a friend to myself if I have a command over my ways of thinking.

Mind is but an instrument

You are using the mind all the time, both to suffer and to accomplish. The mind alone is the cause for bondage and release, *mana eva manuṣyāṇāṁ kāraṇaṁ bandha-mokṣayoḥ...*[9] You are a conscious person who goes about using the mind. The mind is an instrument, *karaṇa*. It does not have independent agenda. You need to have the space to use your mind as an instrument, to take your mind with you. A person who does so is called *ātmavān*, one who has the mind with oneself. When you are frightened, the mind is not with you, but you are with the mind.

---

[7] For whatever reason the unsteady mind, always in a state of flux, goes away, bringing it back from that, with reference to the self alone, may one bring (the mind) into one's own hands (6.26).

[8] *ātmaiva hyātmano bandhurātmaiva ripurātmanaḥ* (*Bhagavad Gītā* 6.5)

[9] *Amṛtabindūpaniṣad* (*mantra* 2)

You are not *ātmavān*. But when you welcome fear, you are *ātmavān*. You need to welcome any emotion; only then you have the choice to be with it or not.

Significance of 108

A certain number of repetitions are advised for *japa* of a particular *mantra* to be efficacious. For instance, the *gāyatri-mantra-japa* has to be atleast twenty-four times because the *mantra* has 24 syllables; one chant for each syllable. If the *mantra* is short, like *oṁ namaḥ śivāya,* then you should chant it 108 times. Merely chanting it for 5 times, on the basis of one chant for each syllable, does not give you enough time to get into the *japa*. For absorption you have to chant until you need to.

The number 108 is significant. All is the Lord. All names are the Lord's name. You cannot repeat all of them, but all names in Sanskrit are between *a* and *h,* the 54 letters. We have to account for all the possible permutations and combinations of these letters. So you count 54 for the ascending and another 54 for the descending order. All combinations are covered, *a-h* and *h-a*. Thus, one *mantra* chanted 108 times symbolically covers all names. When you chant a *mantra* for 1001 or 1008 times, it is symbolic of having done it an infinite number of times.

Prayerfulness

What is 'being' prayerful? It is an attitude of the mind. A prayer is an act and prayerfulness is an attitude. The act of prayer is meant for result, *adṛṣṭa*. It also serves to make you prayerful. You become prayerful when you can assimilate the *dvandva*s, the opposites, both pleasant and unpleasant situations, equally well. You can take them in your stride. You are able to accommodate them with the right attitude. The right attitude serves like a shock absorber against a sense of disappointment and failure. In being prayerful, you can accept your past, and face your present situation objectively. The more prayerful you are, the freer you become from guilt of omission and commission: "I should have done this" and "I should not have done this." You accept situations and learn from your actions.

You also need to be prayerful so that you make the right decisions. Things are not always black and white. Seeing the nuances of a situation and choosing the right course of action is the result of prayer. Assimilating the outcome properly comes from having a prayerful attitude.

Devotion

Becoming a devotee

Bhagavān does not require an act of devotion on our part. Our worship and a song of praise are not going to make him feel better, nor is he someone who is in need of flattery. Anything that we say in his praise is bound to be inadequate. We may use words like omniscient and limitless, but we do not know their real meaning. In our ignorance we say that he is all-knowledge, but what is true is that he is free from ignorance. What could be that mind which is free from ignorance? We have no idea. Yet we use these words in praise. It is like a local villager, who did not complete his elementary education, praising a great mathematician! How is the latter going to be flattered? Anything that we say in praise of Bhagavān is but from our own standpoint. It is like a wave praising the ocean! If we have the devotion, we are not required to act. Why do we act out the devotion in the form of *arcanā, bhajan*, and so on? This is, in a sense, a manner of 'faking it' and in the process 'making it'. By doing so, we discover true devotion.

I can have a deliberate commitment to cultivate devotion. An act comes from my will. If what I do is what I want to do, then there is devotion. If it comes from my own deliberation, it reveals certain disposition. What I do is what is supposed to arise from an accomplished disposition. I will discover that disposition performing those actions that I would perform, if I have the disposition.

A physical action makes an emotion real. Generally, you do not go along with a passing fancy. A fancy, being what it is, passes away. If the fancy repeats itself for a length of time, because of prolonged association with it, it becomes a pronounced desire, "...*saṅgāt sañjāyate kāmaḥ*..."[10] Once it transforms into a desire, then there is a pursuit to fulfill that desire. If you try to satisfy all the desires that you have, you are finished. Fancies come and go. When a fancy repeats itself and you allow that repetition within your heart, you begin liking it. Once it becomes a desire, it is like a bug in your ear; you have to get rid of it. Getting rid of a desire requires that you either fulfill it or grow out of it.

When there is a desire, there is an action on your part, more often than not, seeking to fulfill it. That activity on your part is an expression of a desire in the mind to fulfill what is now no longer a passing fancy, but a *kāma,* demand. Once there is *kāma,* there is action. This action is a physical expression of a desire within. By doing a ritual action you reverse this process. Initially when you perform a ritual, your devotion may be shallow but then it gains depth as you keep the act of devotion going.

---

[10] *Bhagavad Gītā* 2-62

The lord is the creator and I am the created

In the very recognition of Īśvara, the Lord, there is devotion and there is a sense of surrender. The relationship between the Lord and the *jīva* is that of the creator and the created. With reference to the *kārya-karaṇa-saṅghāta,* the physical body-mind-sense complex, the Lord is the cause and I am the effect. As a *jīva* when I see myself endowed with and enjoying this body-mind-sense complex, I become only a *kartṛ*, an agent of action, and the Lord becomes the *karma-phala-dātā,* one who gives the result, the fruits of that action. He is the *karmādhyakṣa,* the one who wields the laws, and I have to go by the laws obtaining in the creation. This relationship is of the creator and the created, and is not variable; it is the same for everyone. My recognition of this makes me a devotee, invariable.

In general, a relevant relationship is recognised by me whenever I associate with a person. Relationships keep changing and are never the same. For instance, attitudinally, with reference to my father, I am a son. When my brother is in my mind, I am no longer the son. I play many different roles with respect to each person that I am related to. When I am the father, I do not behave like a son and when I am the son, I do not behave like a father. Similarly, when I am the brother, I do not behave like a grandson! Thus, every role has a script and each role elbows out every other role. Otherwise, I cannot play any role. It is like acting in a play; I can perform the part of only one role at a time. If this is true with respect to everyone, it is the same for me with respect to the Lord too. Whenever I think of the Lord I become a devotee. When I do not think of the Lord I am not a devotee; then the Lord also becomes like one of my uncles! My attitude reduces the Lord to one of these persons!

Between an individual and the Lord, the relationship is fundamental. If ever there is an absolute relationship, it is between the created and creator. It is not variable. Every other relationship changes circumstantially. I cannot disown this relationship because I am an individual. Even a wise person, a *jñānin,* cannot disown it. He is all-knowledge, *sarvajña,* from the standpoint of the knowledge of reality, *satyaṁ-mithyā,* but with reference to the detailed knowledge, Īśvara alone is both *sarvajña* and *sarvavit*. The *jñānī* has a mind, and with reference to the mind he will say, 'I am a *jīva,* devotee-*jīva,*' all the time because it is an absolute relationship. That is the knowledge. Therefore, when I am father to my son, I am a devotee-father, and with reference to my father, I am a devotee-son. I am a devotee-uncle, a devotee-employer, a devotee-employee, and so on. This is not true nowadays. I am a Sunday-devotee or a Friday-devotee, or a

Saturday-devotee, or a devotee now and then. I have bouts of devotion which fade away. If I am a devotee all the way, the problems of playing a father or a son will not tax the devotee; only the roles have problems.

Relationship with Īśvara is crucial to one's becoming a devotee

If the recognition of the Lord and my being the devotee is complete, then I have opened up. To bring out this devotee in me, I require a program of self-conversion to convert this occasional devotee into an abiding devotee. Meditation, chanting, or performing a ritual can accomplish this. In this way I bring me out of myself. Generally the ego, *ahaṅkāra*, will not be able to offer even a flower unless it gets something out of it. The *ahaṅkāra* asks, "What is it that you are doing?" If I recognise this particular relationship, only then can I do it. By doing an action, an elaborate *pūjā,* in which every action is an offering, the devotion begins to consume the devotee.

Pūjā

Performing a *pūjā* has a cultural background. When you receive a respected guest, culturally, you wash his feet, offer him flowers and receive him inside the home. Then you offer him a seat.

Next, you offer him water and arrange for his bath, give him new clothes, *candana*, and *namaskāra*.

Now, when you wish to worship the Lord, what should you do? You perform the same actions that you do when receiving a revered guest. *Pādya*, you wash the Lord's feet. *Āsana*, you offer him a seat. Then *snāna*, you offer him a bath. After that would come *vastra*-clothes; *ābharaṇa*-ornaments; *candana*-sandal paste; and *puṣpa*-flowers. This is the *upacāra-pūjā*, the steps in propitiation.

Why do you offer flowers and sandal paste? Anything that is fragrant or colorful in the creation is offered to the Lord. What else can you offer? It is all his anyway. You pick the flower and offer it to the Lord because it is fragrant, colorful, and the offering does not deprive anybody. The flowers that are offered are those which would either fall to the ground or wither away on the plant. The flowers of the fruit yielding plants, wherein the fruits are destroyed in the picking of those flowers, are not offered. Certain other flowers are prohibited. In a pumpkin creeper or a variety of squash, the fruit grows first and then the flower appears. You cannot offer that flower.

Sandal paste is, again, a fragrant thing. The whole tree, except the leaf, smells fragrant. This scent never goes away. The wood may not be fragrant on the surface but you just rub it against a rough surface to release its fragrance. It is offered to the Lord and some of it is put on the forehead. The body is a temple. So I offer to my body the same thing that is offered to the Lord.

When you offer flowers to the Lord, you keep saying *namaḥ* each time. *Namaḥ* means my salutation unto the Lord. The flower stands for love and devotion, more a symbol of devotion than love. In devotion there is an awe that He is the Lord. Emotionally there is love. Therefore, both the head and the heart are present in devotion.

While offering flowers and salutations, the Lord is addressed by various names; they may be 12, 16, 108 or 1008 names. In the course of chanting these names of the Lord, the entire scope of Vedanta is covered. Some of the names cover the *mūrta* aspect of the Lord, from the *purāṇa*s, while the other names cover the teachings of Vedanta. Both *saguṇa* as well as *nirguṇa* Brahman are covered. Most of the names, such as *saccidānandāya namaḥ*, *nirmalāya namaḥ*, *ekātmane namaḥ*, and so on, are *lakṣaṇa*s of the *paramātman*. Then there are *saguṇa* names like *sarvajñāya namaḥ*, as well as names connected to the stories that go with the *mūrta*s, forms. These names reveal the nature of Īśvara and also the truth of Īśvara, *paraṁ brahma*.

Further, there is the offering of food, *naivedya*. Afterwards, there is *dhūpa*, incense, and *dīpa*, lighted camphor that is shown while chanting the *mantra* '*na tatra...*'[11]

Then the *namaskāra* is done. There is also some *upacāra*, the singing of the *Ṛgveda*, the *Yajurveda*, and the *Sāmaveda*. Music and dance are also offered.

In the process of this *pūjā*, one discovers an attitude of devotion. The attitude of a devotee is different from the attitude of a layperson; the devotion of a devotee is for knowledge. Knowledge itself is Īśvara and all-knowledge is Īśvara. This attitude brings about a change. Otherwise the heart is rigid. A ritual worship breaks that rigidity because it is an action where there is will and deliberation.

Altar of worship

The altar of worship is more than what your eyes see. If you stand in front of Lord Naṭarāja, wondering what could be the metals in this alloy, and take a picture, there is no altar of worship, it is an object of sense perception. It would take an attitude which is more than perception to see the Lord in this *mūrti*.

---

[11] '*na tatra sūryo bhāti na candratārakaṁ, nemā vidyuto bhānti kuto'yam agniḥ, tameva bhāntam anubhāti sarvaṁ, tasya bhāsā sarvam idaṁ vibhāti.*'

'The sun does not light up that Brahman. The moon and the stars do not light it. These flashes of lightning do not light it. How can this fire light it? Everything shines after that self alone which is light of all lights. By its light all this shines.' *(Muṇḍakopaniṣad 2.2.11)*

If you say it is a bronze, it is perceptual knowledge. But if you say this is the Lord, it is not just perceptual knowledge, you impose the Lord upon it. Every form is a manifestation of the Lord. Any one form does not make the whole. Therefore in any one form you can invoke the whole, like even you invoke the whole ocean in a wave. Touching the wave you can say you have touched the ocean.

Meditation

This worship done at an altar can be done even mentally; when done, it is meditation. *Sajātīya-vṛtti-pravāha,* a continuous flow of thought centred on Īśvara is maintained in meditation, *dhyāna*. The *vṛtti* has to be of the same type, *jāti*. All steps in a *pūjā* have the same *jāti* namely *pūjā*. Even stringing the flowers, decorating the altar with *rangoli* and so on can be included in the *jāti* of *pūjā*. All these, done vividly, mentally, form one action called *dhyāna,* meditation. There are many satellite actions in fire rituals, but they form one *yajña*. Each individual unit produces *apūrva,* unseen result called *utpatti-apūrva,* and these units of *adṛṣṭa* taken together produce the final result, *phala-apūrva*. The same is applicable to any *karma*. For instance in cooking, preparing the vegetables is one unit of action while lighting the stove is another unit and boiling the vegetables in water is yet another unit. Together what you get is the final result, boiled vegetables.

There are various steps involved in performing rituals. Every step is intended for the same purpose and so there is same *jāti*. In the process, you bring out the devotee besides the result of *karma*. What might have passed away as fancy is converted into devotion because of the elaborate physical, oral and mental actions involved.

Love has to be discovered

A loving action grants the condition wherein you discover love. Suppose there is a person for whom you do not have love, you have a dislike. If you want to discover some love for that person, make the effort to give a rose every day for ten days. Soon there will be music inside. Love is not such that it cannot be had. You can love anything; it is a question of granting the condition. When you give a flower, you are granting the condition. You are also willing to grant the condition. Erelong you will discover it. Even though it is a loving action but without love at the beginning, it opens up your heart. What else can you do to get rid of dislike, hatred? You have to do actions that will open you up to make it imbued with love.

In the elaborate process of the *pūjā* that you perform, you discover the fundamental person, the devotee, who plays different roles. If that is understood, the pursuit of *jñāna* is a joyous journey. The difference between the *jīva* and Īśvara makes no difference!

Pūjā helps us gain jñāna

Being a *karma, pūjā* produces result; that is another thing. In the beginning of the *pūjā* you make a *saṅkalpa* for gaining *āyuḥ,* a long life and *ārogya,* a healthy life and so on. Let me enjoy these for the purpose of *jñāna-vairāgya-siddhi,* for the accomplishment of self-knowledge, for which certain objectivity, dispassion, *vairāgya,* is required. Let my *guru* also enjoy good health, and so on, so that he may continue teaching. Thus there is a *saṅkalpa* behind the very ritual whether it is expressed in so many words.

Akhaṇḍa-nāma-japa

Akhaṇḍa-nāma-japa is chanting one *mantra* repeatedly for a length of time. *Akhaṇḍa* means undisturbed or uninterrupted by anything else. You choose any one *mantra* and then you maintain the chant. Some people say that repetition is mechanical, but it depends on what you repeat, and how. Monotony comes only when you want a change. Suppose you commit yourself to not changing your focus, there is no monotony. There is a sense of satisfaction when you are able to do what you are committed to do. When you want to change but you are forced not to, then what is done is monotonous.

There is one great accomplishment in the repetition of *mantra,* chanting for a couple of hours in a group setting. Since it is collective, you have no choice but to chant. Even if you do *akhaṇḍa-japa* alone, it does bring about a change in you. Being oral chanting, you hear what you say. As you say it again, you hear it again, and this goes on. There is only one occupation. This occupation is not separate from you. You become the occupation in *akhaṇḍa-japa.*

Three types of japa

Akhaṇḍa-japa can be *ucca-japa, manda-japa or upāṁśu-japa,* and *mānasa-japa.* In *ucca-japa,* you chant aloud; others can hear you. In *manda-japa,* you and your immediate neighbours can hear your chant, and in *upāṁśu-japa* you can hear, no one else. In *mānasa japa,* you chant mentally. When you chant a *mantra,* you go up, *ucca,* and you go down, *manda.* This kind of chanting in tones that go up and down is generally done in a chorus. This can be done mentally too.

Akhaṇḍa-japa transforms you

In *akhaṇḍa-japa,* you will discover that nothing really bothers you. You can just spend all your time chanting. In fact, you could spend your entire waking life chanting, save the time required for daily routines. In the process you discover that you are acceptably different from what you had taken yourself to be. This kind of chanting just transforms you. This is so because the relationship of an individual, the basic person, to the total is the relationship of the devotee to the Lord. When you chant a given name of the Lord, the innermost person surfaces, not the father, son, brother, uncle, cousin, investor or employee. The basic person related to the Lord assumes all these various roles. When you uncover this basic person, the person and the occupation become one; there is, therefore, absorption called *laya*. This is the trick of rock music too. Even though there is no profound music in rock, there is rhythm which brings about a degree of absorption. Naturally people like the experience. This absorption can put you to sleep too. A child goes to sleep with a soft rhythm, a lullaby. But in *mantra* repetition, the basic person is brought out and there is the wholeness of Īśvara, and if the experience is understood by the teaching of Vedanta, the journey is complete.

This absorption is also healing; it heals the hurt of a person. All the old problems of hurt are healed, being viewed from this absorption of at-homeness. It is not possible for any person in the modern world to be sane without therapy. Everyone has a childhood with unhappy moments. The practice of *japa*, meditation, with understanding of Īśvara heals all the inner hurts. One allows oneself to be covered by Īśvara through the unbroken, *akhaṇḍa,* chanting of Īśvara's name.

Singing also has its own beauty. It too helps the mind. Music has the capacity to bring about *laya,* absorption. *Laya* is healing. To put it in the language of *yoga, sattva-guṇa* is predominanat when one sings in praise of Īśvara. *Rajas* accounts for agitation and *tamas* for dullness as well as veiling. In *rajas* old feelings re-surface. There is healing only when *sattva* is predominant. Real healing is self-healing. Any insight that you gain is *sattva.* This comes about in continuous *nāma-japa.*

You should sit and consciously chant mentally after doing a prayer or a *pūjā,* singing or loud chanting. You have to do it for a length of time for the healing process to begin. It is like having to achieve a minimum threshold of exertion during exercise, to work your heart. So too, only after certain degree of absorption the healing process starts. In addition to this *laya,* there is Bhagavān's grace, because it is a *mantra.*

Mantra Initiation

In the Vedic tradition, *upanayana*, a ritual initiating a student into a *mantra*, initiates a growing person into Vedic studies. One has to be qualified to study the sacred Veda. This is a very important rule that says that unless you are initiated into *gāyatrī* you cannot study the Veda. In fact before teenage, every boy and girl should be initiated into a life of *vaidika-dharma*, which is a life of prayers and duties for self-growth and self-discovery. Once you are initiated into the *mantra*, you are qualified to study the Veda. Initiation is like a rite of passage.

Once you are initiated, you wear the *yajña-upavīta*, the sacred thread, *upavīta*, which commits you to performing Vedic ritual, *yajña*, daily. That is why it is always worn. You cannot throw away this sacred thread until you take up *sannyāsa*. At the time of *sannyāsa*, the thread is thrown away, but the *gāyatrī-mantra* is never given up. This *mantra*, which is an expansion of the *praṇava* or *om*, is collapsed back into the *praṇava* ritually at the time of initiation into *sannyāsa*.

Mantra initiation is also for girls

The *mantra* initiation was originally meant for both boys and girls. Nowadays, marriage is considered to be the *upanayana* for the woman. That is why at the time of the marriage, the man gets one more sacred thread to wear which is of his wife. After marriage he is supposed to perform a two to three-hour ritual daily. Who will prepare the *naivedya*, the food offering, if both of them are at the ritual? The ritual is complete only when food is offered. Therefore, the husband wears the wife's thread so that she can prepare the *naivedya*. That is why she has to come and give him *anujñā*, permission. Both of them start the *yajña*, the ritual, together. Once she gives him the permission, he can continue with the ritual. She will get 50% of the *puṇya*. If he earns any *puṇya*, 50% of it will go to her. If he does something wrong, all the *pāpa* goes to him. If she does anything wrong, 50% of the *pāpa* will come to him. In our *dharma-śāstra*, there is more responsibility for men, and women get due respect. Because she is not given the sacred thread, a woman is not given *gāyatrī*. I believe that both girls and boys need *mantra* initiation to help them into the spiritual journey as a *vaidika*.

Initiation before teenage years

The *mantra* initiation is typically performed between the age of eight and twelve; earlier the better. Before one becomes a teenager, one has enough inner strength gained through *mantra-japa* to see through the difficult teen years to live within the fold of *dharma*.

Traditional initiation includes a ritual of vows also. The boy says, "May I become one conforming to all vows, *sarva vrato bhūyāsam*." This vow is made in the presence of all the relatives attending, the parents, priests, and the sacred fire.

Make your vows public

You have to make your vows public which is why relatives and friends are invited for *upananaya* and marriage ceremonies. You can follow the same principle when you make a *saṅkalpa*. Suppose you want to process your anger, tell everyone at home, "I am not going to victimise anyone when I am angry, from now on." Do not say, "I will not get angry from now on." That is not possible because anger does not take your permission. When it does not take your permission before arrival, you cannot make any decision about its absence in the future. You have no say over what is beyond you. But you can definitely make a commitment with reference to your action because it is based on your free will. If the will is weak, the home members become your support system. Children at home who know your decision would say, "Dad! You are angry now. Let us talk later." "Mom! You are angry now. Let us talk later." Children are very alert in pointing out such things. You find you have an honest home behind you.

Father initiates son into the mantra in upanayana

The initiation begins with taking the blessings of all including the ancestors (*nāndi-śrāddha*) and all the *devatā*s (*udaka-śānti*). Afterwards, the father initiates the son. For this, the father qualifies himself by performing certain rituals and praying for the eligibility to initiate. After performing these rituals he chants the same *mantra* for sometime before he gives the *mantra* to his son. With the blessings of all the ancestors, the *ṛṣi*s, the *devatā*s, and those who have assembled for the function, the initiated child is now qualified to study the Veda.

Japa becomes an inner guide for the initiated

It is very important for a child to have an inner guide in the formative years. An external guide alone is not enough. The child requires inner strength. The initiated *mantra* gives the child an inner strength and certain self-reliance. That is why we make this initiating ritual a big event. When it is done properly, the child understands that it is something very important. When I was given this *mantra* I felt that, 'since so many people had come for my sake, I must be somebody!'

Introducing himself after the *upanayana*, the boy mentions the *ṛṣi* to whom he traces his lineage, *gotra,* and then his *sūtra,* Āpastamba, Bodhāyana, and so on, which state the details of rituals to be performed, their mode of performance and finally the branch, *śākhā,* of the Veda of which he is a student, *adhyāyin.* The word, '*adhyāyin*' has different meanings. The one who wants to study is an *adhyāyin,* the one who is studying is an *adhyāyin* and the one who has studied also is an *adhyāyin.*

There are a few more steps in the *upanayana* ritual. The father tells him, "May you do this *karma* every day with *jala,* water. Do the *ācamanādi-karma.*" He will say, "*bāḍham,* yes." Then, the father tells him, "Do not sleep during the day." He will say, *bāḍham.* Then, "*Ācārya-adhīno bhava,* may you be under the care and guidance of your teacher." He will say, *bāḍham.* "*Karma kuru,* do what is to be done daily." He will say *bāḍham.* After this, the boy is taught the Veda.

The *gāyatrī-upadeśa* comes first because it is as good as being taught the entire Veda. The *mantra* is so complete that even knowing this one *mantra,* you can say, 'I am a *yajuśśākhādhyāyī,*' meaning the one who has studied or is a student of the *Yajurveda.* The word, '*śākhādhyāyī*' is preceded by the name of the Veda, the *Yajus, Sāma, Ṛg* or *Atharva,* the branch which the family has traditionally maintained for centuries. Even though they do not learn the entire Veda, they learn a few significant *mantra*s and recite them while doing *sandhyāvandana* daily. The *gāyatrī-mantra* initiation itself qualifies the boy to say that he is a student of a given Veda even though he is not studying the Veda. That is why to be initiated is a great privilege.

Initiation

One wants to receive a *mantra* from someone for whom one has reverence. One can then put an end to all doubts about which *mantra* one has to chant. Therefore, there is an advantage in getting initiated into a *mantra* by someone in whom one has *śraddhā*. The one who initiates gives the *mantra* that he himself chanted enough number of times. The initiated should do *puraścaraṇa* of the *mantra*, chanting one lakh times for each syllable in the *mantra*. *Gāyatrī* has 24 syllables and so one has to chant 24 lakh times.

Count by time

When doing *puraścaraṇa* counting by time is very good. First, find out how much you are able do in 10 minutes and then chant for the length of time required to do the number of times you have decided to do. The *mantra* is a prayer, and in setting ourselves to chant we are setting ourselves to pray and not merely keeping counts.

Every committed person is eligible for a mantra

Eligibility for a *mantra* comes from one's commitment. If the person has an inclination, *saṁskāra,* and wants to do it then he or she can be given a *mantra.* Nothing else needs to be looked into.

There is a book called *Prapañca-sāra* which contains all the *mantras.* A *mantra* may have a sacred monosyllabic sound, the *bījākṣara. Om* itself is a *bījākṣara.* For each deity, there are certain *bījākṣara-mantras*, like *hrīm* for Śakti and *śrīm* for Lakṣmī. Then there are *mantras* prescribed for certain results. You may want something to happen. The *mantras* for those types of results are different. They are generally *bījākṣaras*. If you are invoking a particular *devatā* of the planets, *navagrahas* like Candra or Sūrya, there are certain *bījākṣara-mantras* for that.

A *kāmya-karma* is performed keeping the limited results in view. Mental chanting, *mānasa-japa,* with this intent is also *kāmya-karma.* As long as it is *kāmya-karma,* the *mantras* are to be chanted with all the required-to-attend disciplines. These *mantras* are to be properly chanted and there is a *niyama,* a rigorous discipline, associated with them which is very difficult to follow these days. Therefore it is irresponsible to give such *mantras* to people who cannot follow all *niyamas.*

There are very effective safe *mantra*s of Śiva, Viṣṇu, Devī, Lakṣmī and other deities; they can be given.

'*Namaḥ,* my salutations unto the Lord,' whether the Lord is Nārāyaṇa, or Śiva or Vāsudeva. It could be *oṁ namo bhagavate vāsudevāya,* the *dvādaśākṣarī-mantra* consisting of twelve syllables, or *oṁ namo nārāyaṇāya,* the *aṣṭākṣarī-mantra* of eight syllables, or *oṁ namaḥ śivāya,* the *pañcākṣarī-mantra* of five syllables. We always add the syllable *gam* for Gaṇapati. We also add *om.* These spiritual *mantra*s are also religious and meaningful. Generally, people want a *mantra* for *japa*-meditation. One of these, or any *mantra* chosen by a knowledgeable person is fine for this purpose. The beauty of these *mantra*s is that we can look into any one of them and get the whole meaning of Vedanta.

Forms of Worship

A few religious theologies are against altars of worship where there are idols installed. They advocate vocal prayer without thinking of the Lord in any form. The mandate is: "Thou shall not worship a form." Even words are symbols, forms. 'Hi' is a form. 'Bye' is a form. When you salute, a message is conveyed through that form. The universe and everything therein are but forms. A particle is but a form, and the macro world of diverse objects is but a form of forms. If the entire universe is a manifestation of Īśvara, every form is Īśvara. You can invoke him in any form. You can invoke him in a *patra*, leaf, by saying, "In this leaf I invoke Īśvara, *asmin patre parameśvaram āvāhayāmi,*" and do *pūjā*. Here the *pūjā* is not for the leaf, it is for Īśvara. It is irrational to think God 'created' the world and has a location in space and time, which themselves are part of creation. The creator of space-time-world cannot sit in space and time! Muchless God can have a location outside space. All locations are within space. The whole *jagat*, whatever that is there including forces, is a manifestation of God. Then every form, every force, every law, is not separate from God. Anything in nature is good enough to invoke the total Īśvara. If you want to touch the ocean, you need not touch the entire ocean! It is neither possible nor necessary.

Touch the wave that comes to your feet; you have touched the ocean.

Everything is sacred

Everything, including your own physical body, is sacred. We have a particular *mantra* that we chant at the end of a ritual.

> यानि कानि च पापानि जन्मान्तरकृतानि च ।
> तानि तानि विनश्यन्ति प्रदक्षिणपदे पदे ॥
>
> *yāni kāni ca pāpāni janmāntara kṛtāni ca,*
> *tāni tāni vinaśyanti pradakṣiṇapade pade.*
>
> May those omissions and commissions done in this life and also in the previous lives and the resulting afflictions perish with every *pradakṣiṇa.*

You do *pradakṣiṇa,* clockwise circumambulation, of the fire in which a ritual was performed and chant this *mantra. Yāni kāni ca pāpāni,* whatever *pāpa*s were done by me in this life and also in the *prārabdha* that I have brought along with me, *janmāntara-kṛtāni ca,* let all of them get neutralised, *pradakṣiṇapade pade,* as I go around you, (oh Lord) in every step. If you have no place to move around the fire, you turn around yourself three times. What does it mean? The body is the temple, *deho devālayaḥ proktaḥ*. And the one who indwells is Īśvara. This is not an ordinary culture.

You need to have some *puṇya* even to know about this, let alone be born into this culture. Everything is Īśvara including what transcends all forms. Then the five elements become objects of worship. We do worship them as the Lord.

Worshipping a form is a blessing

How do you pray, and to whom do you pray, if you do not have any form? Mode of prayer is a form and therefore having an altar for worship is a privilege, a blessing. Every villager knows that everything is God who can be worshipped in any form. Such a heart in a village person reflects the culture of the Vedic vision. Therefore, creating an altar is not a problem for us. Nor do we have any problem when we see people from different cultures offer their prayers differently.

Lord Gaṇeśa

I find that Lord Gaṇeśa is very popular in all our remote villages. Even people from non-Indian traditions like the form of Lord Gaṇeśa because they can relate to it, though they cannot relate to any other form. The form of Lord Gaṇeśa is both human and non-human; it helps people see the whole in the form. The written form of *om* can be seen in the form of Gaṇeśa. The *om* itself cannot be worshipped because you cannot have a form for *om*. It is a sound symbol, a *pratīka,* and not a physical form, a *pratimā.*

Lord Gaṇeśa is the inspiration for every artist. Each one gives you a form unique and beautiful. You cannot worship *oṁkāra* in its written form but you can worship Lord Gaṇeśa which has a form that suggests the written form of *om*.

Lord Naṭarāja

The Lord is seen as being both *amūrta,* one who has no form, as well as *mūrta,* one who is invoked in a specific form. Lord Śiva is invoked in different forms. Each *mūrta* is meant to highlight a particular aspect of the Lord. For instance, the form of Lord Naṭarāja, the *tāṇḍava* Śiva, dancing Śiva, is a *mūrta* that depicts the joy of creation. The cause of creation is *ānanda* and the effect that is dance is not separate from the dancer, the Lord.

In the *Taittirīya Upaniṣad* Varuṇa asks his son Bhṛgu to know that from which everything has come, by which everything is sustained, and unto which everything goes back. At first, Bhṛgu thinks that it is out of *annam,* food, that everybody is born, by food everybody is sustained, and unto food, everybody goes back. If the physical body is taken as being me, this is true. Next, Bhṛgu concludes that *prāṇa,* the vital energy, is the source, Brahman, because mere food does not cause anyone to survive. Then he finds that the *prāṇa* is not Brahman, it is mere energy alone, and that the mind, *manaḥ,* is Brahman. Subsequently, he observes that it is the *ahaṅkāra,* the agent, *kartṛ,* that is Brahman because the mind alone cannot be the cause. Finally, he discovers that *ānanda* is Brahman.

आनन्दो ब्रह्मेति व्यजानात्। आनन्दाद्ध्येव खल्वि-
मानि भूतानि जायन्ते। आनन्देन जातानि जीवन्ति।
आनन्दं प्रयन्त्यभिसंविशन्तीति।

ānando brahmeti vyajānāt, ānandāddhyeva khalvimāni bhūtāni jāyante, ānandena jātāni jīvanti, ānandaṁ prayantyabhisaṁviśantīti.

He knew *ānanda* (fullness) as Brahman; for, from *ānanda*, indeed, all these beings originate; having been born, they are sustained by *ānanda*; they move towards *ānanda* and merge in *ānanda* (*Taittirīya Upaniṣad* 3-6-1).

Until he makes this discovery, Bhṛgu keeps coming back to his teacher Varuṇa for more knowledge. After that realisaton, doubts are no more; Bhṛgu's name is given to the *vidyā* along with the name of his father, *Bhārgavī-Vāruṇī-Vidyā*.

The creation is but a manifestation of *ānanda*. When *ānanda* dances, there is the *jagat* non-separate from the dancer. When there is no dance, the *jagat* is a possibility until the dance begins again. Within the *jagat* also, any creation is born of joy.

The *jaṭā* of Naṭarāja is horizontal, revealing the motion. The flares around are the stars, including our sun. In one hand of Lord Naṭarāja there is fire; fire stands for knowledge. In another hand there is a *ḍamaru;* the *ḍamaru* stands for space and sound, *śabda,* the Veda. The third hand indicates, "Do not be afraid." The fourth points to his feet, "Come to my feet, I will save you." Thus, one can see meaning in every part in the form of Naṭarāja and so too in all forms at the altars of worship.

Śrī Dakṣiṇāmūrti

Lord Dakṣiṇāmūrti is Lord Śiva invoked as a source of all-knowledge; as a teacher of *brahma-vidyā,* knowledge of brahman, knowing which everything is as well known. The form of Lord Dakṣiṇāmūrti itself reveals that all that is there is the Lord.

The Lord as the eight aspects

The Lord is presented in our *śāstra* as one whose manifestation is eight-fold, *aṣṭamūrti.* They are the five elements, the sun, the moon and the person who objectifies them. We know that world is presented by the Veda in the form of these five elements, *ākāśa,* space, which includes time; *vāyu,* air; *agni,* fire; *ap,* water(s),[12] and *pṛthivī,* earth. In this Vedic model of the universe, these five elements constitute the Lord's form which is this universe. The sun and the moon represent the next two aspects. As an individual when I look at this world, what stands out in the sky are the sun and moon. The moon represents all planets and satellites and the sun represents all luminous bodies, the stars. The eighth aspect is me, the *jīva,* who is looking at the world. These eight are to be understood as one whole. This is the Lord.

When you look at the form of Śrī Dakṣiṇāmūrti, there are symbolic features of the five elements. Space, *ākāśa,* is represented by a *ḍamaru,* a drum, in his right hand. In order to show space in a sculpture, it needs to be enclosed. Empty space is enclosed in the *ḍamaru* enabling it to generate sound, *śabda.* Next, *vāyu,* air, is represented by Śrī Dakṣiṇāmūrti's hair with the 'bandana,' the band, holding his hair in place against the wind. *Bandhana* is a Sanskrit word that comes from the root *bandh,* to bind. In his left hand, you will see a torch, which represents *agni,* fire. *Ap,* water, is shown by the Gaṅgā in the form of a Goddess, which you can see on Śrī Dakṣiṇāmūrti's head. *Pṛthivī,* the earth, is represented by the whole idol. Then there

[12] *Ap* (*āpaḥ* in nominative form) is a word that is always plural. It has no singular and dual forms. So, we have indicated in our translation this fact: 'water(s).'

are people, the *jīvas*, Sanaka, Sanandana, Sanātana and Sanatsujāta who are the receipients of knowledge from Śrī Dakṣiṇāmūrti, sitting at the base of the Lord. On the left side of the head of Śrī Dakṣiṇāmūrti you will find a crescent moon, and on the right there is a circle representing the sun. So the five elements, sun and moon with the *jīva* constitute the *aṣṭa-mūrti-bhṛt*, the Lord of eight aspects that are the whole. In reality the *jīva*, the eighth, is the one who is seeing the altar.

The Lord as the teacher

You can worship Śrī Dakṣiṇāmūrti as the Lord, the one who is *aṣṭamūrtibhṛt*, or you can invoke him as a teacher of all teachers. The sitting posture is *vīrāsana* which is a teacher's *āsana*. What does he teach? Look at the gesture of his right hand. His index finger, the one that is used to accuse others, represents the *ahaṅkāra*, the ego. The other three fingers represent your body, *deha*, mind, *antaḥkaraṇa*, and *prāṇa*. They also may be seen as being the three *śarīras*, bodies, the gross, the subtle, and the causal. This is what you take yourself to be. The *aṅguṣṭha*, thumb, represents the Lord, Īśvara. It is away from the rest of the fingers of the hand but at the same time the fingers have no strength without it. In this gesture, *mudrā*, the index finger joins the thumb leaving out the other three fingers to form a circle, teaching that the *jīva*, who takes the self to be as good as just the body, mind, senses and *prāṇa* is, in fact, the whole which has no beginning, no end like the circle. This hand gesture visually depicts the entire *upadeśa,* teaching: "*tat tvam asi,* you are that." This is the last word about you. No theology can improve upon this vision; there is no more whole! Unless you are the whole there is noend for your seeking. I am amazed that such a profound teaching can be shown in a *mudrā,* sign. The source of this teaching, the Veda, is represented by the palm leaves in the left hand of Śrī Dakṣiṇāmūrti.

To understand this teaching, one requires to command compassion and clear thinking. A life lived intelligently, assimilating the value of values and practising the prescribed spiritual disciplines such as daily ritual-prayer, giving, meditation—all these *sādhana*s are represented here by a *japa-mālā.* The fact that the Lord himself is a teacher, a *guru,* means that a teacher is looked upon as a source of knowledge. The teacher should look upon Īśvara, the Lord, as the source of all knowledge. The Lord being the first *guru,* there is no individual ego involved in the tradition of teaching.

There are bound to be obstacles in one's pursuit for this knowledge. That the grace of Śrī Dakṣiṇāmūrti would avoid all possible obstacles is indicated by the figure of Apasmāra with a knife in one hand, being under one foot of the Lord. The Apasmāra is alive, representing all impediments, both internal and external, but he is incapable of striking, being under total control of the Lord. Obstacles may arise, but they would come under check with the grace of the Lord. There is no obstacle-free pursuit, but they need not throw one off the course.

Further, the ear-ring in the left ear is entirely different from the one in the right. The Lord is both male and female and is representing the two causes, the material and the efficient. Both the causes are the same Lord. Thus, the whole form of Śrī Dakṣiṇāmūrti is an altar to invoke the Lord who is the source of all-knowledge, the cause of everything, the one who is the whole, and teaches you are that whole.

Śivaliṅga

The Lord is invoked with the word Śiva and in the form called '*liṅga*' which has no particular form. It includes all forms, making a symbol for the whole. These *liṅga*s are made of different materials. We have *liṅga*s of ruby, emerald, crystal, stone and even of clay.

In Indian logic *liṅga* is a term for *hetu*, cause. *Liṅgyate budhyate anena iti liṅgam*, that with the help of which something is inferred is *liṅga*. For example, smoke becomes the *liṅga* for fire. This is possible because the one who infers knows that there cannot be smoke without fire. With this knowledge of invariable concomitance, *vyāpti-jñāna*, one derives various forms of inference.

If there is a form in which you can invoke Īśvara, who is both the material and efficient cause, the *abhinna-nimitta-upādāna-kāraṇam,* what can be that form? You cannot invoke the Lord in any particular form because it will exclude all other forms. All forms put together would result in a formless form. Suppose out of a ball of wax you create a number of forms, each one separate and different from the others. Now, if you bring them together to a form that includes all forms, you will have a form of no particular form, a *liṅga*. The material cause is non-separate from the creation because the material cause is the creation itself. The creation consists of myriad forms. So we invoke Īśvara who is the creator and the creation, manifest and unmanifest, in the *liṅga*.

Worship of the Five Elements

तस्माद्वा एतस्मादात्मन आकाशस्संभूतः । आकाशाद्
वायुः । वायोरग्निः । अग्नेरापः । अद्भ्यः पृथिवी ।

tasmādvā etasmādātmana ākāśaḥ sambhūtaḥ, ākāśādvāyuḥ, vāyoragniḥ, agnerāpaḥ, adbhyaḥ pṛthivī.

> From that (Brahman) indeed, which is this Self, was born space. From space emerged air. From air was born fire. From fire was created water. From water sprang up earth (*Taittrīya Upaniṣad* 2-1-1).

The five great elements comprise the entire *jagat* as non-separate from Īśvara. Therefore, they command reverence and become altars of worship. In the south of India, there are five Śiva temples known as *pañca-bhūta-kṣetras*, each dedicated to a given element. *Ākāśa*, space, is worshipped as the Lord in the temple of Naṭarāja at Chidambaram. After the *pūjā* they unveil a curtain and show the light of burning camphor. The altar is just space, no form. Space is the *liṅga*. This is the famous secret of Chidambaram; until the 'altar' is understood as space, the altar remains a secret in one's head. The Lord, *cit*, all-knowledge, is in the form of *ambara*, the space.

Vāyu, air, is invoked in the *liṅga* in the temple at Kālahasti, near Tirupati. The main shrine has a lamp burning twenty-four hours, for centuries, whose flame dances all the time because of a continuous draft of air all the time. The constant movement of flame implies the presence of air which is worshipped as the Lord in this temple. There must be a hole which allows only that much air to make the flame only tremulous, but never dead.

Agni, fire, is worshipped in the Aruṇācaleśvara temple in Thiruvannamalai. A flame, *jyoti,* is worshipped there. The hill adjacent to the temple itself is seen as a *liṅga.* A giant lamp with yards of wick and gallons of oil is lighted on a particular day of the year known as *kārtika-dīpam.* The festival attracts thousands of devotees and all of them come to see the Lord in the form of *Agni,* fire.

Ap, water, is worshipped in a temple called Thiruvanikaval near Thirucchirapalli. It is a huge temple and the name of the deity is Jambukeśvara. The *liṅga* is in water that keeps coming into the shrine constantly from a spring, I suppose. The priests need to remove the water from time to time in order to stand there and offer the ritual of worship.

Pṛthivī, earth, is worshipped in the Ekāmbareśvara temple in Kanchipuram near Chennai. The *liṅga* here is a *svayambhū,* a natural form of pure *pṛthivī,* earth. Thus all the five elements are worshipped as the Lord and each one of them has a huge temple.

Mantras and Stotras

Śuklāmbaradharam

शुक्लांबरधरं विष्णुं शशिवर्णं चतुर्भुजम्।
प्रसन्नवदनं ध्यायेत् सर्वविघ्नोपशान्तये ॥

śuklāmbaradharaṁ viṣṇuṁ
śaśivarṇaṁ caturbhujam,
prasannavadanaṁ dhyāyet
sarvavighnopaśāntaye.

I meditate upon (Lord Gaṇeśa), the one who wears a white garment, who is all-pervasive, who has a (bright) complexion like the moon, who has four hands, who has a cheerful face, for the removal of all obstacles.

This is a very popular verse of prayer to overcome *vighnas*, obstacles.

There are obstacles possible in your effort to achieve any desired end. To avoid the obstacles, *vighnas*, you offer a prayer in the beginning requesting that all obstacles be removed. This is a prayer to Lord Gaṇeśa, the one who removes all obstacles.

The word *dhyāyet* should be understood as *dhyāyāmi*, I meditate, because the meaning would be, "May one meditate upon." You are asking yourself to do *dhyāna*, to visualise, think of, and pray. To whom should you pray and why?

Viṣṇum, the one who is *sarva-vyāpī,* all pervasive. This aspect of all pervasiveness indicates that there is no place where he is not. All that is here is Īśvara. If you say he is inside, then the Lord is limited. If you say he is outside, then again, the Lord is limited. However, if you say he is inside and outside, you mean that he is limitless. *Viṣṇuṁ dhyāyāmi,* I salute, I pray to, I meditate upon Viṣṇu, who is all-pervasive.

For the purpose of meditation, we give the Lord a form. *Śaśivarṇam,* he is of the colour of the moon, the autumnal moon. He has four hands, *caturbhujam;* each hand indicating one type of blessing.

Śuklāmbaradhara is the one who wears white clothes. White stands for purity, *śuddha-sattva.* He is the one who is all *sattva,* meaning all-knowledge. *Prasannavadana* is one who has a cheerful face. He is the one whose nature is fullness, *ānanda-svarūpa.*

You will find seeming contradictions in all such descriptions. He is all-pervasive but wears white clothes! He is all-pervasive but one who has four hands! If you look beyond this, you can understand the beauty of it; one is the truth, *svarūpa,* and the other is the form for your visualisation, *upāsana.* You need a form to offer a flower.

Sarva-vighna-upaśāntaye, for the removal of all forms of obstacle. This verse is generally chanted to propitiate and obtain the blessing of Lord Gaṇeśa, the remover of all obstacles.

Agajānana-padmārkam

अगजाननपद्मार्कं गजाननमहर्निशम् ।
अनेकदन्तं भक्तनामेकदन्तमुपास्महे ॥

agajānanapadmārkaṁ gajānanam aharniśam,
anekadantaṁ bhaktānām ekadantam upāsmahe.

We meditate day and night on the one-tusked one who is the sun for the lotus in the form of the face of Pārvatī, the one with the elephant face and the one who is the giver of all desired ends to his devotees.

Gajānanam ekadantam aharniśam upāsmahe. Gaja is elephant and *ānana* means face. *Gajānana* is one who has the face of an elephant. *Ekadanta* is the one who has only one *danta,* tusk. *Upāsmahe* means we meditate upon and *aharniśam* means day and night. We meditate day and night upon that one who has the face of an elephant, and who has one tusk.

Agajānana-padmārkam is a compound word. That which is born is *jaḥ, jāyate iti jaḥ. Gaḥ* means that which goes, *gacchati iti gaḥ. Agaḥ* means that which does not move, *na gacchati iti agaḥ, parvata,* mountain. The king of the mountain is *parvata-rājā. Agāt jāyate,* then, is the one who is born of *aga,* the mountain king. This is Goddess Pārvatī. Pārvatī is called Agajā, Girijā. In this context *agajānanam* is *agajāyāḥ ānanam*, the face of Goddess Pārvatī. This face of Pārvatī is likened to the lotus, *padma, agajānanam eva padmam.*

For a lotus to bloom, the presence of the sun is required. While the water-lily blooms in the wake of moon at night, the water-lotus blooms only when the sun is up. *Arka* means sun. So too Pārvatī's lotus like face requires a sun to bloom, and this is Lord Gaṇeśa. He is the one who is the sun, as it were, for the lotus that is the face of Goddess Pārvatī. When she sees Lord Gaṇeśa, she is so happy that her face blossoms. Lord Gaṇeśa is himself *gajānana,* who has the face of an elephant which is a symbol for all wisdom and all power.

What is *anekadantam*? It is *anekadaṁ tam*. The one who gives is *daḥ, dadāti iti daḥ*. The one who gives *ekam*, one thing, is called *ekadaḥ, ekam dadāti iti ekadaḥ*. Lord Gaṇeśa is not the giver of only one thing. He is *anekadaḥ*, the giver of all that you want; in the second case-ending, it is *anekadam*. He gives *aneka*: *dharma, artha, kāma,* and *mokṣa*. You can get everything by his grace. *Tam* means him. *Anekadaṁ tam* means unto that Lord whose grace will help you achieve everything. For whom is he *anekadaḥ*?

Bhaktānām, for his devotees, those who invoke him. We meditate upon this Lord Gaṇeśa.

Yā kundendu

या कुन्देन्दुतुषारहारधवला या शुभ्रवस्त्रावृता
या वीणावरदण्डमण्डितकरा या श्वेतपद्मासना ।
या ब्रह्माच्युतशङ्करप्रभृतिभिर्देवैः सदा पूजिता
सा मां पातु सरस्वती भगवती निश्शेषजाड्यापहा ॥

yā kundendutuṣārahāradhavalā yā śubhra-vastrāvṛtā
yā vīṇā-varadaṇḍa-maṇḍitakarā
yā śveta-padmāsanā,
yā brahmācyuta-śaṅkara-prabhṛtibhir-devaiḥ sadā pūjitā
sā mām pātu sarasvatī bhagavatī niśśeṣajāḍyāpahā.

Sarasvatī, Bhagavatī, is of fair complexion like the necklace which is as white as the jasmine, moon and snow, who is dressed in white clothes, whose hands adorn the divine *vīṇā*, who is seated on a white lotus, who is always worshipped by Gods like Brahmā, Viṣṇu, Śaṅkara. May she, who removes the darkness of ignorance, protect me!

Yā sarasvatī sā māṁ pātu: One who is the Goddess of knowledge, Sarasvatī, *sā māṁ pātu*, may she protect me! She is further described:

Yā–one who is; *kunda-indu-tuṣāra-hāra-dhavalā*: of fair complexion (*dhavalā*) like the necklace (*hāra*) which is as white as the jasmine (*kunda*), moon (*indu*), and snow (*tuṣāra*); *yā śubhra-vastrāvṛtā*: *śubhra-vastra* means white garments. *Śubhra-vastreṇa-āvṛtā*, the one who wears garments that are white in colour; *yā vīṇā-vara-daṇḍa-maṇḍitakarā*: one whose hands adorn the divine *vīṇā*; *yā śveta-padmāsanā*: one who is seated on the white lotus, *śveta-padma*; *yā brahma-acyuta-śaṅkara-prabhṛtibhiḥ devaiḥ sadā pūjitā*: *yā*, tho one who is, *sadā pūjitā*, always worshipped, *brahma-acyuta-śaṅkara-prabhṛtibhiḥ*, by Gods like Brahmā, Acyuta (Viṣṇu) and Śaṅkara, all these *devatā*s revel in the knowledge that she represents, and the lesser Gods, seek that knowledge.

Sā Bhagavatī, that *īśvara-śakti* as Goddess of knowledge; *niśśeṣa-jāḍyāpahā*: *apahā* is the one who destroys or removes. What does she remove? *Jāḍya*, ignorance, *tamas*, dullness. She is the one who removes the dullness in the *buddhi* which denies the clarity of knowledge. She removes all distorted perceptions with reference to the realities about oneself and about the world. *Śeṣa* means left over; *niśśeṣa* means without anything being left over, that is, totally. She removes all doubts completely. That is why Lord Kṛṣṇa says,[13] "In this world, there is indeed no purifier equivalent to knowledge."

---

[13] *Na hi jñānena sadṛśaṁ pavitram iha vidyate*... (*Bhagavad Gītā* 4-38)

Iha, here, in this world, *na vidyate*, it is not there, *jñānena sadṛśam*, equal to knowledge, *jñāna*.

Fire, water, and a variety of things purify, but there is nothing that can purify your heart except knowledge of the self that is already pure. This knowledge removes not only the present problems but also all the problems you had created before. It removes *saṁsāra*. Within *saṁsāra* all other things may purify, but this *jñāna* of the self purifies you from *saṁsāra* itself which is an impurity, *mala*. "...The fire of knowledge reduces all actions (results of actions) to ashes."[14] That is why Goddess of knowledge Sarasvatī is described as being *niśśeṣa-jāḍyāpahā*. May the Goddess Sarasvatī, the remover of the entire darkness of ignorance, who is described thus, protect me.

Gāyatrī-mantra

ओं भूर्भुवस्स्वः। तत्सवितुर्वरेण्यं
भर्गो देवस्य धीमहि। धियो यो नः प्रचोदयात्॥

oṁ bhūrbhuvaḥ svaḥ, tat-saviturvareṇyaṁ
bhargo devasya dhīmahi, dhiyo yo naḥ pracodayāt.

Om, the Lord, is earth, the space in between and the heavens. That Lord is the one who is the most worshipful. We meditate on that

---

14 ...*jñānāgniḥ sarvakarmāṇi bhasmasātkurute* (*Bhagavad Gītā* 4-37)

effulgent, all-knowledge Lord. May he set our intellects in the right direction.

The *gāyatrī-mantra* is an excellent prayer. The sense of the prayer is, "May the Lord brighten my mind and make me think properly so that I make proper decisions." Life is a series of decisions, big and small. Wrong decisions result in your being in the wrong place or in the right place, but at the wrong time. You are successful when you are in the right place at the right time. But nobody knows what the right place is, or when it is the right time. It all depends upon your decisions. Sometimes it is difficult to know what is right and what is wrong; it is confusing. Therefore, you require clarity and inner leisure to make decisions correctly so that you do not act impulsively. Generally one would pray for knowledge, a job, money, power and so on. But this is not such a prayer. This prayer is only for clarity of thinking. Everything else will come if clarity is there. If Goddess Sarasvatī is there, Goddess Lakṣmī is bound to come. Sarasvatī makes it possible to acquire Lakṣmī.

Nevertheless, Lakṣmī takes away all our time and energy. The entire time of a human being is consumed at the altar of Lakṣmī. Money, including real estate, is Lakṣmī, Dhanalakṣmī; it means the happiness born out of money. Lakṣmī does not mean mere money. Money can bring sorrow too.

Lakṣmī is the happiness born of money. Food is Lakṣmī, Dhānyalakṣmī or Annalakṣmī; marriage is Varalakṣmī. Then you have a Gṛhalakṣmī, having a home and domestic happiness. Children are Santānalakṣmī. Any success is Jayalakṣmī. Dhairyalakṣmī is courage, enterprise and so on. So all the important things in life such as money, job, health, food, home, marriage and children, are all Lakṣmī.

Even though you may have all of this, but unless Goddess Sarasvatī is also present, you cannot enjoy any of them. Therefore you invoke Sarasvatī first. That is the mark, *lakṣaṇa*, of a real Hindu. You have to have your priorities clear about what signifies real *sampat*, wealth. Once you have that, everything will come to you. Even if you have nothing else you can still be happy sitting under a tree. This is the essence of the *gāyatrī-mantra*.

Gāyatrī is the name of a *chandas*, metre, consisting of 24 syllables, having three *pāda*s, lines, unlike '*dharmakṣetre kurukṣetre samavetā yuyutsavaḥ...*' (*Bhagavad Gītā* 1-1) that has four quarters being *anuṣṭubh-chandas*. Gāyatrī is the name of the *mantra* as well as the metre. This *mantra* is in all the four Vedas ad therefore it is the most sacred and popular among the *mantra*s for initiation. The deity of the *mantra* is Savitrī. The *gāyatrī-chandas* is used only in the Veda, and there is a *mantra* set in the *gāyatrī-chandas* for every *devatā*.

All the *gāyatrī-mantras* end with *pracodayāt*. The word, '*dhīmahi*' will also be there in every one of them.

Oṁ bhūrbhuvassvaḥ: *Om* is the Lord. We invoke the Lord as the source of all blessings, as the one who protects and sustains this world. The Lord is equated to all the three worlds, *bhūḥ*, *bhuvaḥ* and *svaḥ*. Because these words are in apposition, *sāmānādhikaraṇya*, to one another, they refer to the same substantive. *Om* is *bhūḥ*, the earth. *Om* is *bhuvaḥ*, everything above the earth. *Om* is *svaḥ* or whatever is beyond our mind, beyond the scope of our perception. *Om* is a part of the *mantra*. *Bhūrbhuvassvaḥ*, which is only an explanation of *om*, is not part of the *mantra*.

Tad vareṇyam: That *vastu om* is indicated by *tat*. *Vareṇyam* is *varanīyam*, the one to be worshipped, to be invoked, and whose blessing is to be sought.

Savituḥ devasya dhīmahi : *Dhīmahi*, we invoke. The verb *dhīmahi* is in the plural because the one who prays includes all others in his or her prayer. Both, *savituḥ* and *devasya* go together; they are in the sixth case. It means we invoke that Lord, *devasya*, the effulgent being who is in the form of *savitṛ*. *Savitṛ* means the sun, standing for the whole cosmos. We invoke that Lord who is in the form of *savitṛ-maṇḍalam*. We dwell upon that Lord who is also like the *savitṛ*, the sun, who is all-effulgence. Just as the sun is free from darkness, so too is the Lord all-knowledge, one who is free of ignorance. Here, we invoke that Lord.

Yaḥ bhargaḥ: *Bhargaḥ* means the one who burns all ignorance, confusion. Therefore, he the all-knowledge *bhargaḥ*, who burns all my confusion, *naḥ dhiyaḥ pracodayāt*. *Naḥ asmākam* our, *dhiyaḥ*, minds, *pracodanaṁ kuryāt*, may brighten. *Pracodanam* also means set. May the Lord set our minds to proper thinking so that we make proper decisions in our life. The prayer is: "May our ways of thinking lead to right decisions, may we have our minds under our control, and may we think properly." While in the beginning the *gāyatrī-mantra* is a prayer, later it becomes a *mantra* for contemplation.

Oṁ namo bhagavate dakṣiṇāmūrtaye

ओं नमो भगवते दक्षिणामूर्तये ।
मह्यं मेधां प्रज्ञां प्रयच्छ स्वाहा ॥

oṁ namo bhagavate dakṣiṇāmūrtaye,
mahyaṁ medhāṁ prajñāṁ prayaccha svāhā.

Om. Salutations to Bhagavān Dakṣiṇāmūrti. (Oh Lord) Bless me with memory, the capacity to think properly, and clarity, wisdom.

Namaḥ, my salutations, to the Lord, Bhagavān, the one who has *bhaga*, the six-fold glories—*aiśvarya*, overlordship; *śrī*, wealth and health; *vīrya*, strength;

yaśas, fame; *jñāna*, knowledge, and *vairāgya*, freedom from a sense of want. The word 'Bhagavān,' by which I invoke the Lord, is everything that I seek. Not only do I seek *mokṣa*, knowledge, I also seek blessings for achieving whatever I need to achieve in life. Therefore, in relating to the Lord as Bhagavān, I am invoking the grace of Bhagavān.

Amūrtiḥ is the one who is formless and who is the truth of everything. With *māyā-śakti* Īśvara is *dakṣiṇaḥ*, the one who has the capacity to be the creator and sustainer, and also the one who can take back the whole creation into himself. Therefore, Īśvara who is *dakṣiṇa* as well as *amūrti* is Dakṣiṇāmūrti.

Dakṣiṇa also means the southern direction. He is the Lord who is facing the south, *dakṣiṇa-dik-abhi-mukhā mūrtiḥ*. What is the significance of the southern direction? The north attracts, and it stands for *mokṣa*. The south stands for *saṁsāra*; it is Lord Yama's place. The Lord is everywhere, but the one who wants release from *saṁsāra* faces the Lord in the north. The Lord has to face you to teach. As the source of all-knowledge, he faces the south. Salutations unto Lord Dakṣiṇāmūrti who is the source of all-knowledge and the source of all blessing.

Mahyam, to me, *prayaccha*, give; what? Asking is important. Always ask for what do you want. Often we hear, "Do not ask Bhagavān. He knows everything.

He knows what do you need." Asking is part of prayers, as a *karma*. Bhagavān's grace is always available, but you have to tap it. This grace is like ground water that has to be tapped by the act of prayer.

Gaining anything in terms of worldly or spiritual life depends upon your making the right decisions. Life is a series of decisions. You are what you are because of your decisions. For making the right decisions you require two things, *prajñā*, clarity of knowledge and *medhā*, availability of memory. In understanding any topic, you require *prajñā*. It means alertness, clarity of vision. No matter what the topic is, whether it is a moral issue, a legal issue, or an economic issue, to succeed you require *prajñā*.

Medhā, thinking power and memory has to be at service always. Memory is important. If *medhā* and *prajñā* are there, all success will come to you. That is why you pray, "Oh Lord please bless with me with *medhā* and *prajñā*."

Svāhā is a word used at the time of offering oblations unto fire for different *devatā*s. Here the meaning would be, "This chanting is my offering to you."

Maunavyākhyā

Lord Dakṣiṇāmūrti is described beautifully in this *dhyāna-śloka*, meditation verse:

मौनव्याख्याप्रकटितपरब्रह्मतत्त्वं युवानं
वर्षिष्ठान्तेवसदृषिगणैरावृतं ब्रह्मनिष्ठैः ।
आचार्येन्द्रं करकलितचिन्मुद्रमानन्दरूपं
स्वात्मारामं मुदितवदनं दक्षिणामूर्तिमीडे ॥

maunavyākhyāprakaṭitaparabrahma-
tattvam yuvānaṁ
varṣiṣṭhāntevasadṛṣigaṇairāvṛtaṁ
brahmaniṣṭhaiḥ,
ācāryendraṁ karakalitacinmudram
ānandarūpaṁ
svātmārāmaṁ muditavadanaṁ
dakṣiṇāmūrtimīḍe.

I salute Śrī Dakṣiṇāmūrti, who is not subject to time, who makes known the truth of Brahman through the implied meaning of words, who is surrounded by disciples who are themselves *ṛṣi*s and committed to the knowledge of Brahman, who is the teacher of teachers, whose hand is held in the gesture of widom, whose nature is fullness, who revels in himself, and who has a smiling face.

Mudita-vadanam, the one who has a smiling face. The teacher cannot look very serious when he is teaching that you are *ānanda*. He is sitting there under this tree with a smile. *Svātmārāmam*, the one who is reveling in himself, who is *ānandarūpam*, in the form of *ānanda*. *Ānanda* is not necessarily laughing;

there can be quiet, smiling *ānanda* too. *Karakalita-cinmudram,* whose hand is held in the gesture of wisdom, *cinmudrā*.

Varṣiṣṭhāntevasad-ṛṣigaṇairāvṛtam, surrounded by a group of elderly sages, (Sanaka, and others), who are *brahmaniṣṭhas*, committed to the knowledge of Brahman. *Ācāryendram,* the initiator of all the teaching is the Lord, Indra, of the teachers. They say Śrī Dakṣiṇāmūrti taught in silence. If you are the *sanakādi-jīvas*, then, perhaps, silence is enough. If silence were the teaching, then these *upaniṣads* will have empty pages instead of text. The teaching is in the form of words. *Mauna-vyākhyā-prakaṭita* means what is taught is the intended meaning of the words, *śabda-lakṣya,* and not the immediate meaning, *śabda-vācya*. The teaching negates wrong notions you have about yourself. When the negation is complete, you remain as the very *lakṣya,* the target, the meaning that the words want to convey. The teaching is such that you recognise yourself, dropping all your wrong notions. That is what they call *mauna,* silence.

Yuvānam, here, means timeless, *nitya-yuvā,* the one who is not subject to time. He is always young. He faces the south and the students face the north. This is one meaning of Dakṣiṇāmūrti. Another is the one who has all the capacity, *dakṣiṇaḥ,* and is formless, *amūrtiḥ, dakṣiṇaścāsau amūrtiḥ*.

He is *dakṣiṇaḥ*, the one who has capacity to be both the maker and the material cause. He is the creator, the sustainer and the one who takes everything back into himself. The idea here is that the Lord is both the manifest and unmanifest *jagat, dakṣiṇaḥ*. But in truth he is without form, *svayam aṁūrtiḥ*. Therefore, the *jagat* is the Lord whose essential form is free from *jagat*. That is what he teaches.

Nidhaye sarvavidyānām

निधये सर्वविद्यानां भिषजे भवरोगिणाम् ।
गुरवे सर्वलोकानां दक्षिणामूर्तये नमः ॥

nidhaye sarvavidyānāṁ bhiṣaje bhavaroginām,
gurave sarvalokānāṁ dakṣiṇāmūrtaye namaḥ.

Salutations to Śrī Dakṣiṇāmūrti, the reservoir of knowledge, the healer of all those who suffer the disease of *saṁsāra* and the teacher of the whole world.

Nidhi means treasure-house or reservoir. *Nidhaye* is in the dative case which gives the meaning, unto the treasure-house, reservoir. Of what? *Sarvavidyānām*, of all knowledge.

Bhiṣaje bhavaroginām. A *bhiṣak* is doctor. The Lord is considered to be a doctor. He is the Vaidyanātha, the Lord of physicians. For what kind of disease? The *bhavaroga*, the disease of 'becoming,' which is *saṁsāra*. *Bhavaḥ eva rogaḥ, bhavarogaḥ,* a life of becoming alone is disease whose cause is self-ignorance. The Lord is the physician who cures the people suffering from the disease of *saṁsāra*; unto him the treasure-house of all-knowledge, *nidhaye, namaḥ,* salutations. Salutation unto the one who is the healer, whose grace removes this disease of *saṁsāra,* a life of becoming.

Gurave sarvalokānām. The word *gurave* means unto the *guru,* the teacher, who is *sarvalokānāṁ guru,* the teacher of all teachers. He is the *jagad-guru,* the one who is the source of all knowledge and who is the teacher of all. Unto that Dakṣiṇāmūrti, (my) salutations.

Oṁ namaḥ praṇavārthāya

ओं नमः प्रणवार्थाय शुद्धज्ञानैकमूर्तये ।
निर्मलाय प्रशान्ताय दक्षिणामूर्तये नमः ॥

oṁ namaḥ praṇavārthāya
śuddhajñānaikamūrtaye,
nirmalāya praśāntāya
dakṣiṇāmūrtaye namaḥ.

Om. Salutation to the one who is the meaning of *praṇava,* who is in the form of pure knowledge, who is taintless and who is free from any change. To that Śrī Dakṣiṇāmūrti, (my) salutations.

Om is an invocation to the Lord. *Praṇavārthāya*. Unto *praṇavārtha,* the meaning of *praṇava. Praṇava* is the name of *om,* but we do not chant in *japa, praṇava, praṇava... Praṇava* means always fresh or eternal which is *om* and *artha* is meaning. So *praṇavārtha* is the meaning of *om*. The meaning of *om* is Bhagavān, the Lord, and is derived from the root *av,* which means 'to protect'– *avati rakṣati iti om. Om* is the one who protects and sustains the entire creation.

Śuddha-jñāna-eka-mūrtaye. Eka-mūrtaye, unto the one who is *eka-mūrti,* of one form, of unsullied knowledge. The Lord is in the form of knowledge which is unsullied by ignorance, who is also essentially pure consciousness, the self, *ātman*.

Nirmalāya, unto the one who is free from any kind of wrong or right actions, *pāpa* or *puṇya,* and unto the one who is full and complete, *praśāntāya,* always being resolved in his glory; unto him my salutation.

Īśvaro gururātmeti

ईश्वरो गुरुरात्मेति मूर्तिभेदविभागिने ।
व्योमवद्व्याप्तदेहाय दक्षिणामूर्तये नमः ॥

īśvaro gururātmeti mūrtibhedavibhāgine,
vyomavadvyāptadehāya dakṣiṇāmūrtaye namaḥ.

Salutations to Lord Dakṣiṇāmūrti, who is all-pervasive like space but who appears (as though) divided as Lord, teacher, and the self.

The Lord himself is in this three-fold form as Īśvara, *guru* and *ātman*, the self. *Mūrti-bheda-vibhāgine*, the one who remains 'as though' divided in this three-fold form. Like what?

Vyomavad vyāpta-dehāya. Vyomavat, like space. Like the space inside your stomach, the space inside the room and the space outside pervades everything, so too, the reality of Brahman pervades the Lord, Īśvara, the *guru*, and the individual, the *jīva*. Salutations unto the one whose form, *deha*, is all-pervasive like space, and who is nothing other than the *saccidānanda* Brahman.

Tatpuruṣāya vidmahe

ओं तत्पुरुषाय विद्महे। महादेवाय धीमहि। तन्नो रुद्रः प्रचोदयात्॥

oṁ tatpuruṣāya vidmahe mahādevāya, dhīmahi tanno rudraḥ pracodayāt.

Om. May we know that Lord Īśvara, for which may we meditate upon Mahādeva. May that Rudra impel us (towards him).

Rudra is the one who is known through the *śāstra*s or Vedas. The word 'Rudra' means the one who destroys *saṁsāra* or *ajñāna,* ignorance. The other meaning is the one into whom the whole world is resolved. When the Lord absorbs into himself everything that is projected, he is Rudra. That is why you will see Lord Śiva sitting in meditation. Everything is absorbed into him; the whole world of time and space collapses into him. The limitless conscious being, *saccidānanda-vastu,* who is Īśvara as the one who brings into manifestation, sustains and resolves the world, *sṛṣṭi-sthiti-laya-kartṛ,* is called Rudra, in the function of resolving. He is the one whose grace is invoked for the removal of ignorance. This Rudra is *puruṣa,* who is *pūrṇa* or limitless. What kind of *puruṣa* is he?

Tatpuruṣāya, tasmai puruṣāya which is to be taken as *taṁ puruṣam.* It is told in the *śāstra*s that Īśvara, is the *prathama-puruṣa,* the first person. In English grammar what we call the third person is the first person in Sanskrit. He is the first one and everything comes from him. We pray to know that being, *puruṣa,* who is *pūrṇa,* limitless, and who is revealed by the *śāstra. Puruṣāya* is construed as *puruṣam,* the accusative case.

Vidmahe, may we know or come to know. The verb is in the plural. This is a *gāyatrī-mantra.* In all *gāyatrī-mantra*s, like this one, the verb is in the plural. Why do we say 'we' when it is 'I' who wants to know? This is because we include others in our prayer. May we know that *puruṣa* who is limitless.

Mahādevāya dhīmahi. *Dhīmahi* means we meditate upon. We meditate upon that Lord Mahādeva who is *mahān*, limitless, and who is all-knowledge *deva*, the Lord of all Lords and the Lord of all *devatā*s like Indra, Varuṇa and so on.

Tat, that Rudra or Mahādeva, who we want to know and upon whom we meditate, *naḥ pracodayāt*, may he impel us. May he set our minds in the proper direction to enable us to discover what the truth is, and what the Lord is. Here one meaning of *pracodayet* is, may he impel the mind on the proper course of action. We can also understand it to mean *pracodanaṁ kuryāt*. *Pracodana* means *dyotana*, illumination. May he endow our minds with lustre and clarity, may he make all our thoughts brilliant or effulgent!

Rājādhirājāya

ओं राजाधिराजाय प्रसह्यसाहिने । नमो वयं
वैश्रवणाय कुर्महे । स मे कामान्कामकामाय मह्यम् ।
कामेश्वरो वैश्रवणो ददातु । कुबेराय वैश्रवणाय । म
हाराजाय नमः ॥

oṁ rājādhirājāya prasahyasāhine, namo vayaṁ
vaiśravaṇāya kurmahe, sa me kāmānkāmakāmāya

mahyam, kāmeśvaro vaiśravaṇo dadātu, kuberāya vaiśravaṇāya, mahārājāya namaḥ.

Om. We offer (our) salutations unto the Lord, the king of kings, the satisfier of desires. May the Lord of desires give me, the seeker of desires, what I desire. Salutations unto the Lord, the great king, the Lord of wealth.

Mahārājāya namaḥ, salutations unto that Lord who is the king of all kings, the emperor, the *mahārāja.* All kings depend upon him. The *jīvas*, even if they are kings, are all dependent upon Īśvara, but Īśvara is one who is not dependent; he is *mahārāja.*

Rāja-adhi-rājaḥ. There are many kings, *rājās*. Amongst them, he is the *adhi-rāja. Rājānam adhikṛtya rājā bhavati,* on whom all the *rājās* are centred, presiding over all the kings, he is the king; or from the standpoint of all the kings, he is the real king.

Prasahya sāhine. Prasahya means totally, absolutely. *Sāhine,* to the one who is absolutely pleased with himself. It is because of this that he is the *rājādhi-rāja,* king of all kings.

Namo vayaṁ vaiśravaṇāya kurmahe. Namo is *namaḥ,* salutations to him, *tasmai namaḥ.* Vaiśravaṇa is the one who is in the form of Indra, the king of the heavens, the king of all bounty, rains, etc. *Vayam* is we. *Vayaṁ kurmahe namaḥ,* we offer our salutations, *vaiśravaṇāya,* to Vaiśravaṇa.

Saḥ me kāmān kāma-kāmāya. Saḥ means he, that Lord, Īśvara, and *me* means me. What kind of me? *Kāma-kāmāya,* the desiring me; the one who desires a variety of objects. That which is desired is the object, *kāmyate iti kāmaḥ. Kāmānāṁ kāmaḥ,* the desirer for objects is called *kāma-kāma. Saḥ me kāma-kāmāya,* unto me who is the desirer of objects, *dadātu,* may he give, or let him give. May he give all the objects of desire, *kāmān dadātu.*

Who is he? *Kāmeśvaraḥ, kāmānām īśvaraḥ,* the Lord of all *kāma,* desires and objects of desire. You cannot ask anybody else for the fulfillment of your desires. You can ask only the owner of everything. Only the Lord can give everything to us because, being the creator, everything belongs to him. Therefore he is Kāmeśvaraḥ, the Lord of all objects who is also in the form of objects. Vaiśravaṇa, Indra is only symbolic, an *upalakṣaṇa,* for all the Gods. Indra also means the Lord of the heavens.

Kuberāya vaiśravaṇāya mahārājāya namaḥ. Salutation unto the Lord of wealth, Kubera, the son of Viśravas, who is the king of kings. Lakṣmī is the real money but she appoints Kubera as the presiding deity of money. What you want to gain here in this world is the power of Kubera and what you want to gain in heaven is the power of Vaiśravaṇa, Indra. Therefore, you have the words *mahārājāya namaḥ,* which means salutations unto that *mahārājā,* the king of all kings, the Lord who is in the form of Kubera and Vaiśravaṇa. There is only one Lord. All Gods are this one Parameśvara who assumes these different forms from different standpoints.

Na tatra sūryo bhāti

न तत्र सूर्यो भाति न चन्द्रतारकं
नेमा विद्युतो भान्ति कुतोऽयमग्निः ।
तमेव भान्तमनुभाति सर्वं
तस्य भासा सर्वमिदं विभाति ॥

na tatra sūryo bhāti na candratārakaṁ
nemā vidyuto bhānti kuto'yamagniḥ,
tameva bhāntam-anubhāti sarvaṁ
tasya bhāsā sarvamidaṁ vibhāti.

Neither does the sun shine there, nor the moon with all the stars, nor does this lightning shine. What to say of this fire? Everything shines after him who alone shines. By His light all this shines variously.

Tatra, there, *na sūryo bhāti,* the sun does not shine, and *na candra-tārakam,* where the moon does not shine with all the stars.

Na imāḥ vidyutaḥ bhānti, where even the boastful lightning flashes do not enter. *Kutoyam agniḥ,* what to talk of the fire that I am showing you? The sun is bright because my eyes are capable of sight. If my eyes do not see, they are not bright any more. The sun illumines, but my eyes illumine the sun too. My eyes illumine because my mind illumines the eyes. My mind is shining because of the self, *ātman*, which lights up everything. This self lights up my mind, my senses and the whole world. That light is self-effulgent. It is in the form of *caitanya*, consciousness. What is the source of the *ātman*?

It does not need borrowed light; it is self-effulgent. Such is his *svarūpa*. *Tatra sūryaḥ na bhāti*, *sūrya* does not illuminate the self, without whom *sūrya* himself would not shine. The Lord is not the object of any illumination. It is he who illumines everything.

When I show *ārati*, I want to light up the light of all lights with this camphor light. It is like holding a candle in front of the sun to illumine it! He is the light of all lights because of which the mind thinks, my eyes see, my ears hear, and the sense of smell, taste and touch, all perform their functions. I want to light up that light with this light. *Kutaḥ agniḥ*, what is this flame of lamp going to do? Yet I am lighting it because it symbolises the light of knowledge. In ignorance, everything is hidden. The light of knowledge dispels that darkness of ignorance.

Tameva bhāntam anubhāti sarvam—anubhāti means shines after; that alone shines in which everything shines after.

Tasya bhāsā sarvam idaṁ vibhāti, it is because of his light alone that everything, including the mind and the senses, shines.

Śrīrāma rāma rāmeti

श्रीराम राम रामेति रमे रामे मनोरमे ।
सहस्रनाम तत्तुल्यं रामनाम वरानने ॥

śrīrāma rāma rāmeti rame rāme manorame,
sahasranāma tattulyaṁ rāmanāma varānane.

In chanting his name again and again, '*śrīrāma rāma rāma*,' I discover joy in Lord Rāma who pleases my heart and whose face is a blessing. His name is equal to the one thousand names of Lord Viṣṇu.

This is a wonderful verse and a *mantra* worth chanting daily.

The word 'Rāma' comes from the root *ram* which has the meaning of playing, reveling, being joyful, *ramu krīḍāyām*. The one in whom people discover joy is Rāma, *ramante yasmin iti rāmaḥ*. The word '*rāma*' was there long before Lord Rāma came. The word, '*kṛṣṇa*' was also there before Śrī Kṛṣṇa came.

The verb in this verse is *rame. Ahaṁ rame*, I revel in joy. In what do I discover this joy? *Rāme*, in Lord Rāma, *manorame*, in the one who pleases my mind, my heart. *Manorame rāme ahaṁ rame*, I discover joy in Lord Rāma who pleases my heart.

How do you revel? *Śrīrāma rāma rāmeti japan rame*, I discover joy, repeating Lord Rāma's name. *Sahasranāma tat tulyam. Tulyam* means equal to. The name of Rāma is equal to the *sahasranāma*, the one thousand names of Lord Viṣṇu. You do not need to read the *sahasranāma*. Just one word 'Rāma' is enough. This is called *praśaṁsā*, praise. When you are praising Lord Rāma's name, the *Viṣṇu-sahasranāma* is seen as being nothing in comparison! Similarly, when you praise the *sahasranāma*, you elevate it and describe it as being better than everything else.

Varānane goes with *rāme. Rāme varānane*, to think of his face is itself a blessing for me. *Varam ānanaṁ yasya*, that *ānana*, the face of Lord Rāma, is a blessing. Because it is *upāsya*, an altar of meditation and prayer, it becomes the *varānana*, the face that is a blessing. *Varānane rāme manorame aham rame śrīrāma rāma rāmeti*, in chanting his name again and again I discover joy in Lord Rāma who pleases my heart and whose face is a blessing.

Namaste astu bhagavan

नमस्ते अस्तु भगवन् विश्वेश्वराय महादेवाय त्र्यम्ब-
काय त्रिपुरान्तकाय त्रिकालाग्निकालाय कालाग्निरुद्राय
नीलकण्ठाय मृत्युंजयाय सर्वेश्वराय सदाशिवाय
श्रीमन्महादेवाय नमः ॥

namáste astu bhagavan viśveśvarāyá mahādevāyá tryambakāyá tripurāntakāyá trikālāgnikālāyá kālāgnirudrāyá nīlakaṇṭhāyá mṛtyuñjayāyá sarveśvarāyá sadāśivāyá śrīmanmahādevāya namáḥ.

Oh Lord, may this salutation be unto you who is the Lord of the universe, limitless and effulgent, all-knowledge, the one who projects, sustains and takes back this universe, the one who is timeless and also the destroyer of time, all-pervasive, the conqueror of death, the Lord of all, and the ever auspicious one who is always a blessing.

This is a beautiful *mantra*. It is very good, especially for *prāyaścitta*, and can be chanted when one feels guilty for one's omissions and commissions.

Namaḥ, salutations. *Te,* to you, *astu*, be. Bhagavan, Oh Lord! My *namaskāra* unto you!

Namaḥ astu viśveśvarāya: You have to repeat *namaḥ astu* with each name. *Viśveśvarāya*, Īśvara, the Lord of the entire *viśva*, world is called Viśveśvara. My salutations unto the Lord of the entire world.

Mahādevāya: Unto the one who is *mahān*, limitless, and a *deva*, effulgent.

Tryambakāya: Unto the one who has three eyes. He knows the past, the present and the future. He is all-knowledge.

Tripurāntakāya: Unto the one who is *antaka,* the one who brings an end of *tripura,* the three *puras*, cities or worlds, *bhūḥ, bhuvaḥ* and *svaḥ. Tripurāntaka* is the one who takes all the three worlds unto himself.

Trikālāgni-kālāya: Unto the one who devours the three *kālas*, time—past, present and future. *Kālaḥ eva agniḥ kālāgniḥ, kāla* itself is *agni. Agni* means fire. *Kālāgni,* time, is such that like even fire it devours everything, and the Lord devours time itself. In other words, the Lord is timeless, being the creator, the sustainer, and the destroyer of time.

Kālāgnirudrāya: He is *kāla-agni-rūpeṇa rudraḥ,* the one who, in the form of the *kāla-agni,* time, makes everybody weep. It means he is the chastiser, the giver of the fruits of action, *karma-phala-dātṛ*.

Nīlakaṇṭhāya: Unto the one whose *kaṇṭha,* neck, is the blue sky, who is all-pervasive and manifest in the form of the *jagat*. This is a beautiful vision of the whole *jagat* as a manifestation of Īśvara, with the blue sky being Bhagavān's neck.

Mṛtyuñjayāya: Unto the overlord of *mṛtyu,* death. The Lord of Death thought that he was the greatest, until he was made to realise that Īśvara was supreme.

There are many interesting stories about this. The story of Mārkaṇḍeya is based upon this aspect of Īśvara.

Sarveśvarāya: Unto the Lord of all the worlds, *bhūḥ, bhuvaḥ* and *svaḥ*. He is the Lord of all beings, including the various *devatā*s, deities.

Sadāśivāya: Unto the one who, despite being the Lord of everything, is himself untouched by anything. The entire *jagat* is his manifestation, sustained by him and absorbed back unto him, but who is he? He is *sadāśiva,* of the nature of pure *ānanda,* the limitless Consciousness.

Śrīman-mahādevāya namaḥ: My salutations unto the one who is *śriman-mahādeva. Śriman* is *śrimat,* which means *śrimān,* one who is a blessing. In reciting this verse, I invoke the Lord in the form of *śriman-mahādeva* and seek his blessing.

Śivamānasapūjā

The entire form of worship is done mentally in *Śiva-mānasa-pūjā.* Whatever is performed with the prescribed steps in a typical *pūjā* is done mentally, but very vividly, as though it is done physically. Doing mentally is meditation with its own *dṛṣṭa* and *adṛṣṭa* results.

There is a beautiful story associated with a temple in Tirunindriyur near Chennai. It seems that the king of that kingdom built a temple and set a day for its *pratiṣṭhā*, consecration. A few days before the consecration he had a vision in which he saw a *sādhu* sitting under a tree, and there was a message that the *sādhu* had built a temple and was having its consecration on the same day and at the same time as that of the temple built by the king. A consecration ceremony is always performed at certain auspicious time and on certain auspicious day, and there are not many such days available. You get an appropriate day only once every few months. That is why many marriages take place on the same day during the same *muhūrta*, chosen auspicous time. Hindu religious life is highly controlled by the Hindu calendar.

In the story, both the king and the *sādhu* had chosen the same day and the same time for consecration and therefore the message was that the king should postpone his consecration ceremony. The king wondered how a *sādhu* could build a temple in the same region without his knowledge. So he searched for the *sādhu*. He then saw the tree and the *sādhu* sitting under it, just as he had seen in his vision. So his vision was not wrong. He asked the *sādhu*, "Have you built a temple? The *sādhu* said, "It is almost over. I am giving it the finishing touches." "Where is the temple?" "Oh, it is in my mind. I have been building it for the past 10 years!" He had been building a temple in his mind, brick by brick, for ten years, vividly remembering how much he had accomplished the previous day and picking up from there! Now he was giving it the finishing touches. The king said, "It seems your temple is more important than mine. I have also built a temple, but the Lord seems to be more interested in your temple." The *sādhu* said, "I have been building this temple for ten years without anyone's help, while you have been building a temple with the help of people. That is why the Lord is interested in my temple." The king wanted to know the plan of the *sādhu*'s temple. The *sādhu* told him that he would give him the plans after its consecration. On being given the *sādhu*'s plan, the king remodelled his own temple according to that design. That temple still stands today near Chennai.

So, the *pūjā* that is performed physically at an altar can also be performed mentally. When you are doing *pūjā* mentally, you can pick up a flower at will. When you do it for real, you need to fetch the flowers. You can do the *pūjā* quite vividly in your mind. You get certain insight into the ways of thinking too. Besides that, it generates a condition for discovering the devotee in you. You are a devotee. Just as you become a swimmer by swimming, you can become a devotee by being devout. The *Śivamānasapūjā* has a cultural overtone, naturally, because Śrī Śaṅkara composed it. The method of worship is based on how it is done in India.

रत्नैः कल्पितमासनं हिमजलैः स्नानं च दिव्याम्बरं
नानारत्नविभूषितं मृगमदामोदाङ्कितं चन्दनम् ।
जातीचम्पकबिल्वपत्ररचितं पुष्पं च धूपं तथा
दीपं देव दयानिधे पशुपते हृत्कल्पितं गृह्यताम् ॥ १ ॥

ratnaiḥ kalpitamāsanaṁ himajalaiḥ
snānaṁ ca divyāmbaraṁ
nānāratnavibhūṣitaṁ mṛgamadā-
modāṅkitaṁ candanam,
jātīcampakabilvapatraracitaṁ
puṣpaṁ ca dhūpaṁ tathā
dīpaṁ deva dayānidhe paśupate
hṛtkalpitaṁ gṛhyatām. (1)

I mentally offer you a throne studded with precious stones, a bath with Gaṅgā water, celestial robes inlaid with many gems, sandalwood paste mixed with musk to anoint the body, jasmine and *campaka* flowers, and *bilva* leaves, burning incense and a shining flame. Oh, self-effulgent Lord, ocean of compassion, and the lord of all living beings, may you receive what I offer with all my heart and my mind! (1)

An altar is created in your own mind. You can start with this *mānasa-pūjā* every day when you begin your contemplation. *Ratnaiḥ kalpitam āsanam,* I offer to the Lord, *āsana,* a seat. *Āsyate asmin iti āsanam,* wherever one is seated it is called an *āsanam*. What kind of *āsanam* is this? It is *kalpitam*, studded, *ratnaiḥ*, with precious stones. It is after all a mental offering. Why should you be a miser when you are offering only in the mind? You can give any kind of *āsanam* you want.

Himajalaiḥ snānam: *Himajala* is snowmelt, which is the river Gaṅgā. Pots full of water from the Gaṅgā are offered. You always offer only that which you feel good about, anyway. You could also say that you offer *uṣṇodaka*, warm water, if you prefer that. It is possible to do that mentally.

Nānāratnavibhūṣitaṁ divyāmbaram: *Ambara* is the clothing, *vastra*. *Divyāmbara* is celestial apparel, whatever it is. It is not something *laukika*, of our world, but a wonderful fabric. The whole outfit is *divyāmbara*. It is *vibhūṣitam*, decorated with many gems, *nānā-ratnaiḥ*.

Mṛgamadāmodāṅkitaṁ candanam: *Mṛga* is deer. *Mada* is what is born of that. On certain gum trees, you can see that the gum seeps out and dries on the bark of the trees. That is called the *mada* of the tree. It is an expression in Sanskrit. The *mṛgamada* is the musk, also called *kastūri* which is born of the deer. *Āmoda* is fragrance. *Candana* is sandal paste. This sandal paste is made more fragrant, *āmodita-aṅkitaṁ candanam*, by mixing it with musk. At the Tirupati Bālāji temple they mix *candana* and *kastūri*.

In every temple, this adorning, *alaṅkāra*, is an act of devotion. When the Lord is decorated, they put together a number of items. It is just like the dressing table of a very rich and sophisticated lady where there are bottles everywhere. The priests do the *alaṅkāra* behind closed curtains. Flowers are offered next.

Racitaṁ puṣpam: *Racitam* is a garland and *puṣpam* is flower. What flowers are they? *Jātīcampaka-bilvapatram. Jātī* is a kind of a jasmine: while the jasmine is a plant, the *jātī* is a creeper. *Campaka* is another beautiful yellowish flower. This grows on a tree. The *bilva* is also the leaf, *patra*, of a tree. Its fruit is medicinal. The leaf is also a curative for stomach ulcers. There are such purāṇic stories associated with certain flowers, leaves and so on.

Dhūpam is incense. *Dīpam* is burning camphor. You show the light of the camphor to the Lord. It is lit with the flame of the lamp that is there around. Even in *mānasa-pūjā*, you should be very careful when you light the camphor, like you would in a real *pūjā*. In that light, you see the reflected face of the Lord.

Deva dayānidhe paśupate: *Deva*, the one because of whom all the lights shine. Oh self-effulgent Lord, *dayānidhe*, the one who is a treasure-house, storehouse, *nidhi* of *dayā*, ocean of compassion. He is the ocean of *dayā*. *Paśupate*, the one who is the Lord of *paśu*, the Lord of this body.

Hṛtkalpitam. Hṛdā kalpitam. Hṛt means *hṛdaya*, heart. *Hṛdayena, manasā*, with my mind and all my heart, *kalpitam*, what is offered, *gṛhyatām*, may you receive. What is offered, let it be received. This is the first verse. The *naivedya* is the next step.

सौवर्णे नवरत्नखण्डरचिते पात्रे घृतं पायसं
भक्ष्यं पञ्चविधं पयोदधियुतं रम्भाफलं पानकम्।
शाकानामयुतं जलं रुचिकरं कर्पूरखण्डोज्ज्वलं
ताम्बूलं मनसा मया विरचितं भक्त्या प्रभो
स्वीकुरु ॥ २ ॥

sauvarṇe navaratnakhaṇḍaracite
pātre ghṛtaṁ pāyasaṁ
bhakṣyaṁ pañcavidhaṁ payodadhi-
yutaṁ rambhāphalaṁ pānakam,
śākānāmayutaṁ jalaṁ rucikaraṁ
karpūrakhaṇḍojjvalaṁ
tāmbūlaṁ manasā mayā viracitaṁ
bhaktyā prabho svīkuru. (2)

Pāyasa made with clarified butter in a golden bowl inlaid with the nine precious stones, the five kinds of snacks, banana and fruits with milk and curd, many vegetables, clean and tasty water, betel leaf and nut mixed with camphor—all of this I offer to you mentally with great devotion. May you receive them, Oh Lord! (2)

What you first offer to the Lord is sweet. The first thing that they serve on a banana leaf is a little bit of sweet. If there is no sweet they will at least serve some sugar just to begin with. One is supposed to eat that first. The sweet that is dessert will come in its own turn, in due course. *Ghṛtaṁ pāyasam* is a sweet porridge made with ghee, clarified butter. How do you offer the *pāyasa*? *Pātre,* in a cup. What kind of cup is it? It is not a paper cup. *Sauvarṇe navaratna-khaṇḍaracite. Sauvarṇa* is that which is made of *svarṇa,* gold. The *navaratna* are nine precious stones. *Khaṇḍa* is pieces and *racita,* here, means inlaid. Whether the *pāyasa* is tasty, you serve it in a very attractive cup! It is a golden cup inlaid with the nine precious stones.

Bhakṣyaṁ pañcavidham: *Bhakṣyam* is what is masticated and eaten, crunchy. There are five types, *pañcavidham,* of *bhakṣyam* offered here. *Payodadhiyutaṁ rambhāphalam* is banana with milk and yogurt. *Pānaka* is sweetened water.

Śākānām ayutam: *Śāka* means vegetables and *ayutam* is many. (Actually it means 10,000.) *Jalaṁ rucikaram*: *jalam* is water, *rucikaram* means clean, tasty water.

Karpūrakhaṇḍojjvalaṁ tāmbūlam: *Tāmbūlam* is the betel leaf and nut. It is a kind of mouth freshner that is chewed after lunch. Here you are offering *tāmbūlam* mixed with camphor.

Mayā manasā viracitaṁ bhaktyā: All of this is *viracitam*, offered to you, *mayā manasā*, by me, mentally, in my thoughts, and *bhaktyā*, with great devotion. *Prabho svīkuru*, may you receive it, Oh Lord! I offer this to you with great devotion.

छत्रं चामरयोर्युगं व्यजनकं चादर्शकं निर्मलं
वीणाभेरिमृदङ्गकाहलकलागीतं च नृत्यं तथा।
साष्टाङ्गं प्रणतिः स्तुतिर्बहुविधा ह्येतत्समस्तं मया
सङ्कल्पेन समर्पितं तव विभो पूजां गृहाण प्रभो॥ ३॥

chatraṁ cāmarayoryugaṁ vyajanakaṁ
cādarśakaṁ nirmalaṁ
vīṇābherimṛdaṅgakāhalakalā-
gītaṁ ca nṛtyaṁ tathā,
sāṣṭāṅgaṁ praṇatiḥ stutirbahuvidhā
yetatsamastaṁ mayā
saṅkalpena samarpitaṁ tava vibho
pūjāṁ gṛhāṇa prabho. (3)

A pair of fans, an umbrella, a spotless mirror, musical performance of *vīṇā*, *bheri* and *mṛdaṅga*, followed by a dance performance, an *aṣṭāṅga-namaskāra* and this manifold praise—all this I offer to you with my *saṅkalpa*. May you please receive this worship, Oh Lord, the one who pervades everything! (3)

Cāmara is a pair of fans that is soft. It is made out of an animal's tail that is very soft. *Vyajanaka* is another kind of fan. The *chatra* is an umbrella. All these are part of worship, *upacāra*.

Nirmalam ādarśakam: This is a spotless mirror. You show a mirror as if to ask the Lord, "Is everything okay? Please see for yourself."

Vīṇābherimṛdaṅgakāhalakalāgītaṁ ca nṛtyaṁ tathā: Then you offer him *gīta*, a music performance accompanied by *vīṇā*, a string instrument, *bheri*, lute, a wind instrument and a *mṛdaṅga*, which is a percussion instrument. This music is followed by dance, *nṛtyaṁ tathā*.

Sāṣṭāṅgaṁ praṇatiḥ. Praṇati is prostration. *Sāṣṭāṅga* means with all the eight *aṅgas*, limbs, touching the ground. This is also called the *aṣṭāṅga-namaskāra*, '*padbhyāṁ karābhyāṁ jānubhyām urasā śirasā vapuṣā vacasā manasā caiva praṇāmo'ṣṭāṅga ucyate*.' *Padbhyām*, with the feet, *karābhyām*, with the hands, *jānubhyām*, with the knees, *urasā*, with the chest, *śirasā*, with the head, *vapuṣā*, any part not mentioned, meaning the stomach, *vacasā*, by words and *manasā*, by thought. I offer my prostrations thus, unto you.

Stutirbahuvidhā hi etat samastaṁ mayā samarpitam: all these manifold praises are indeed offered by me with devotion. *Tava vibho pūjāṁ gṛhāṇa prabho*:

please receive this worship, offered unto you, oh Lord, the one who pervades everything.

आत्मा त्वं गिरिजा मतिः सहचराः प्राणाः शरीरं गृहं
पूजा ते विषयोपभोगरचना निद्रा समाधि-स्थितिः ।
सञ्चारः पदयोः प्रदक्षिणविधिः स्तोत्राणि सर्वा गिरो
यद्यत्कर्म करोमि तत्तदखिलं शम्भो तवाराधनम् ॥ ४ ॥

ātmā tvaṁ girijā matiḥ sahacarāḥ
prāṇāḥ śarīraṁ gṛhaṁ
pūjā te viṣayopabhogaracanā
nidrā samādhisthitiḥ,
sañcāraḥ padayoḥ pradakṣiṇavidhiḥ
stotrāṇi sarvā giro
yadyatkarma karomi tattadakhilaṁ
śambho tavārādhanam. (4)

My I-sense, *aham*, is you. My mind is *pārvatī* wedded to you. My five organs of action and five physiological functions are your servants. My body is a house for you. I offer you all the pleasures of my senses. My sleep is a state of resolution in you. Whenever I walk, I am going around you. Anything I utter is in praise of you. Whatever I do is a form of worship unto you, Oh Lord! (4)

For the Lord this body is a temple. The devotee makes his or her own body a temple now. *Ātmā tvam*, whatever the I, *aham*, is, *tvam*, you are that. The mind, *matiḥ,* is Girijā, you are the *puruṣa* and she is the *prakṛti*. *Girijā-matiḥ,* my mind is Pārvatī, who is wedded to you. *Sahacarāḥ prāṇāḥ*. The *prāṇa*s are all the *karmendriya*s, organs of action, the organ of speech, hands, legs, and so on, and also the *pañca-prāṇa*s, the five physiological functions. They are *sahacarāḥ,* your servants. They go along with you. *Me śarīram,* my body, is a *gṛham,* the house for you. Oh Lord, you are seated in it as the *ātman*.

Te pūjā, to you this is my *pūjā*. What *pūjā*? All the *viṣayopabhogaracanā,* all these various objects, enjoyments and all forms of experiences are a form of worship of you, like the flowers that we offer at your feet. All the objects that I perceive through my sense organs, or infer with my mind, and whatever I see or hear, all of them fall at thy feet. Let them be as though offering of flowers to you.

Nidrā, my going to sleep is the equivalent of your *samādhi*. You are always in *samādhi*. I am with you in my *nidrā*.

Padayoḥ sañcāraḥ pradakṣiṇavidhiḥ: The movement of my legs and feet are my doing *pradakṣiṇa,* religious circumambulation to you.

Stotrāṇi sarvā giraḥ: When you are the *ātman* and my mind is Girijā, then anything that I say is going to be *stotra*s, about thy glory alone. All my words, *sarvā giraḥ,* are thy glory. I do not lose sight of you.

Yadyatkarma karomi, whatever *karma* I do, *Śambho*, Oh Lord, *tattadakhilam*, all of it is, *tavārādhanam*, worship unto you.

करचरणकृतं वाक्कायजं कर्मजं वा
श्रवणनयनजं वा मानसं वापराधम्।
विहितमविहितं वा सर्वमेतत्क्षमस्व
जय जय करुणाब्धे श्रीमहादेव शम्भो ॥ ५ ॥

karacaraṇakṛtaṁ vākkāyajaṁ karmajaṁ vā
śravaṇanayanajaṁ vā mānasaṁ vāparādham,
vihitam avihitaṁ vā sarvametat kṣamasva
jaya jaya karuṇābdhe śrīmahādeva śambho. (5)

Whatever omissions and commissions I have performed with my hands, legs, speech, body, sense organs, organs of action, and mind, whatever I may have done with reference to enjoined or prohibited actions, please forgive them all, Oh Lord Mahādeva, Oh ocean of compassion! (5)

Karacaraṇakṛtaṁ karmajam, born of whatever action I have performed with my legs and hands; *vāk-kāyajam*, whatever I have done either orally or by the use of my limbs; *śravaṇa-nayanajam*, anything born of my sense organs such as ears, eyes, and so on; *mānasam*, whatever action I have done mentally. An *aparādha* is an omission of the right action or commission of the wrong.

Vihitam avihitaṁ vā, whatever I have done with reference to *vihita-karma* or *avihita-karma*. *Vihita* is what is enjoined, *avihita* is *niṣiddha*, prohibited action. *Karuṇābdhe sarvam etat kṣamasva*, may you forgive everything Oh Lord, the ocean of mercy!

Saha nāvavatu

स ह नाववतु । स ह नौ भुनक्तु । सह वीर्यं करवावहै ।
तेजस्विनावधीतमस्तु । मा विद्विषावहै ॥
ओं शान्तिः शान्तिः शान्तिः ॥

sa ha nāvavatu, sa ha nau bhunaktu, saha vīryaṁ karavāvahai, tejasvināvadhītam astu, māvidviṣāvahai.
oṁ śāntiḥ śāntiḥ śāntiḥ.

May he (the Lord) protect both of us. May he nourish both of us (with knowledge). May both of us make effort for the capacity (for knowledge to take place). May what is studied by us, be brilliantly clear. Let us not have any misunderstanding. Let there be freedom from three possible obstacles.

Sa ha nāvavatu. Saḥ ha nau avatu. Saḥ means Īśvara, the Lord. So, may the Lord *ha*, definitely, indeed, *avatu*, protect and bless, *nau*, both of us.

The word *om* is also derived from the same root as *avatu*, the root *av*. *Av* is used in the sense of protecting. *Om* means the one who protects being a source of blessing. Thus the Lord's name is *om*. You can also say he is the one who sustains everything. May that Lord bless both of us, teacher and student.

Sa ha nau bhunaktu. Saḥ, that Lord, *ha*, definitely, indeed, *bhunaktu*, nourish, *nau*, both of us. The root *bhuj* in the verb *bhunaktu* is also in the sense of protection. It does not mean eating here; in that case, the verb would have a different ending, the *ātmanepada* ending.[15] The sense here is only of nourishing. May he nourish both of us with knowledge. May the Lord indeed, ignoring all my omissions and commissions, being blind to them, bless us and nourish us both. Both, student and teacher, seek Bhagavān's blessing.

Saha vīryaṁ karavāvahai. Saha, together, *karavāvahai* (may we) exert for *vīrya, sāmarthya* (capacity to gain knowledge). Whatever is required to gain this knowledge, may we make an effort for that. On the part of a student the capacity consists of certain conditions, commitment, *śraddhā*, background knowledge, the power of retention and recollection.

---

15 *bhuṅgtām*

The teacher also needs commitment, health, time and so on. May we both enjoy the respective required qualifications.

Tejasvināvadhītam astu: *tejasvi nau adhītam astu.* Whatever *śāstra* is studied, *adhītam*, by both of us, communicated by one and gained by the other, let it not remain mere words; *astu*, let it be *tejasvi*, meaningful, *nau*, for us. *Tejas* means brilliance. Let the understanding not be vague, but brilliant like the sun that is not obscured by the clouds. You cannot miss the sun even when the clouds are there. It is not like inference in which you infer the presence of the sun upon seeing the silver lining of the clouds. The *śāstra* is not a matter for inference. It is 'I' and has to be understood very clearly. Therefore, let what is studied be brilliantly clear, free from any vagueness, much less error.

Mā vidviṣāvahai: A *dveṣa* is any kind of dislike or misunderstanding. May we not be subject to this misunderstanding. Let nothing come in between us so that this communication is complete.

Oṁ śāntiḥ śāntiḥ śāntiḥ: We chant *śānti* three times. There are not three types of *śānti.* There is only one *śānti*, but there are three types of problems that can deny *śānti*. Let there be freedom from those problems. Let problems not arise from the forces over which we have no control, *ādhidaivika*; from the beings around us, *ādhibhautika;* or from factors centred on ourselves, *ādhyātmika.* The first set of problems comes from sources over which we have no control whatsoever, like cyclone. We can only protect ourselves from it. Let there not be obstacles from such sources over which we have no control. That is one *śānti.* The second source of *aśānti* is any kind of disturbance from the external world, political, social or domestic which is an obstruction to our pursuit. We pray for *śānti* from these obstacles that we do not want to have. The third *śānti* is to take care of problems centred on oneself. There can be physical problems, like an inability to sit comfortably for some time, physiological problems like indigestion, and so on. The mind itself can pose a problem.

I pray that all the three capacities, physical, *deha;* physiological, *prāṇa;* and mental, *manaḥ,* be available to me in a manner that is conducive to my pursuit of this knowledge, *vidyā.* In chanting these three *śānti*s, I pray for freedom from these three possible obstructions.

Om

Om is a profound, single-syllable word. *Om* represents the underlying order that sustains all that is here; it is the name of the Lord. One invokes the Lord through *om*. This is why many of the prayers, chants and *mantra*s begin with *om*. There is a reference to the significance of *om* in the *Kaṭhopaniṣad* (1-2-15):

सर्वे वेदा यत्पदमामनन्ति
तपाꣳसि सर्वाणि च यद्वदन्ति ।
यदिच्छन्तो ब्रह्मचर्यं चरन्ति
तत्ते पदꣳ संग्रहेण ब्रवीमि ओमित्येतत् ॥

sarve vedā yatpadamāmananti
tapāṁsi sarvāṇi ca yadvadanti,
yadicchanto brahmacaryaṁ caranti
tatte padaṁ saṅgraheṇa bravīmi omityetat.

All the Vedas talk about which goal, to know which, people take to a life of study and spiritual discipline, I tell you in brief—that is *om*.

There are many who live a studious and disciplined life devoted to the contemplation of the ultimate goal. That which they seek is *om*.

Om as a word

In Sanskrit, *om* means that which sustains, or that which protects, *avati, rakṣati*. We understand that which sustains or governs everything to be the order, which, going a step further, is the reality of everything. *Om* is the essence of that order. This means *om* is the name of the Lord who pervades everything in the form of the order that sustains.

When we say that order is behind everything, we do not mean that it is literally 'behind' anything that is here. We mean that it is everything that is here. For instance, what I hold in my hand is a cup. What makes it a cup? Why does it serve a particular purpose and not any other? Why is its material, stainless steel, not subject to rusting? It is order that makes a thing what it is. It is because of the order that this cup is a cup. This form is retained by the order. Its material is maintained by the order. Anything that is here is pervaded by this order.

What you see is the object and what you can sense is the order. This order is Īśvara. The object itself represents order. This is a steel cup today, and you can call it a steel cup tomorrow as well. Therefore, it is in order. If, tomorrow, it were not a steel cup, it would still conform to the order. For example, you see the form of a flower today. A few days later there is no flower; a fruit is there instead. That is also order. Order implies that all things are as they are. Everything is maintained by the order, called *niyati*. That *niyati* is Īśvara, the Lord, and the meaning of *om*.

भूतं भवद्भविष्यदिति सर्वमोङ्कार एव।

bhūtaṁ bhavad-bhaviṣyad-iti sarvamoṅkāra eva

What had been, what is now and what will be—everything is just *om* (*Māṇḍūkyopaniṣad*, 1).

In communication, a word, *abhidhāna*, conveys its meaning, *abhidheya*. The word used for an object and the object are the same. In other words one cannot think of the word without thinking of its meaning. For instance, if I say, 'pot,' the pot-object will come to your mind. If you do not know the meaning of the word, it will not be a word to you, but a sound or a group of sounds. Once you know the meaning of a sound or a group of sounds, you have a word and therefore its meaning is not separate from the word.

Thus, *om*, for those who understand its meaning, is the truth of the Lord. *Om* is not, as they say, the primordial sound. *Om* is the name for the Lord who is everything. When I say the word *om*, if you understand its meaning, you can see that it is non-separate from the Lord.

Om as a sound-symbol

The whole *jagat*, the manifest world, is seen as being one, but looking at it severally, you can say it has countless forms. You can look at each one of these forms as one thing, but if you look at it individually, you find that it is a combination of many other things. Each of these has a form for which you give a name. For instance this physical body is one, but severally it has various limbs; there are two hands, ten fingers, two legs, ten toes and so on. Within each part, there are many cells. If you take the cells, you see that they are all different such as liver-cells, brain-cells etc. Then each of these cells have further components like DNA and so on. Thus, you you keep on finding components within component; there are so many different forms within each form.

The various names and forms are not separate from the Lord; they are the Lord. If I have to give the Lord a name so that I can relate to him, what name should that be? Should it not be a name that includes all forms? When I say 'pot' it does not mean a chair, and neither is it a table, a tree, or a carpet. It only means pot. The Lord is the one who is pot, chair, table, tree, carpet—everything. Therefore, the name for the Lord should be a name that includes everything, that conveys the same meaning in every language, every dialect. Also, there are many objects in the world that are not yet known; we keep on inventing new gadgets for which we discover new names.

When looking for a word, the Sanskrit language presents another problem. It is full of compound words, and it is possible to keep creating such compounds which are valid words that will not be found in any dictionary. Linguistically speaking, giving a name to the Lord who is all names and forms is an impossible task. Because this name cannot be related to language, we do not look at it as a word. Instead, we look at it as something purely phonetic.

All names are nothing but words. All words are nothing but letters, and all letters are, in turn, nothing but sounds. The letters and alphabets themselves are unique to each language and therefore different in each. For instance, the English alphabet is from 'A' to 'Z,' and the Latin alphabet begins with 'Alpha' and ends with 'Omega'. The Sanskrit alphabet goes from '*a*' to '*h*'. Therefore, to cross the individuality of languages, we have to look beyond letters.

Beyond letters, a name becomes a group of sounds. When you do not know a language, you hear only sounds. In every language, certain sounds repeat themselves and are the unique characteristic of that language. But whatever may be your language, when you open your mouth and make a sound effortlessly, the sound that is produced is '*a*'. If you close your mouth and make a sound, the sound is '*m*'. There is no other sound possible after closing the mouth. Every other sound whether a vowel or a consonant, lies between the '*a*' and '*m*' sounds. One sound that can represent all the other sounds and, in a sense, round-off all the sounds, is produced when you round your lips and make a sound. The sound will be '*u*'. I combine these three sounds '*a*,' '*u*,' and '*m*' and make a single syllabic sound symbol *Om*. Phonetically '*a*' + '*u*' is 'o'.

Om is, thus, a sound symbol, *pratīka*, to denote the Lord who is everything in the entire universe. When we say that *om* is everything, we mean the Lord is everything. Also the Vedas superimpose the entire *jagat* upon the three phonetic parts of the syllable, *om*.

The letter '*a*' stands for the entire physical world of your experience. When you are awake, you are aware of your physical body and this physical world. You are also aware of the experience of the physical world. At the same time, you are aware that you are the experiencer. All the three, the experienced, experience, and experiencer, that you are aware of are the sound '*a*'.

The letter '*u*' is the thought-world which is as distinctly experienced as the physical world. This thought-world is experienced by all while dreaming, and also fantasising while awake. The object of the thought world and the experience thereof, with the experiencer, are superimposed upon the sound '*u*'.

Then there is the letter '*m*'. It stands for the experience in deep sleep, the unmanifest condition of world of experience.

Thus, the waker and the waking experience, the dreamer and the dream experience, the sleeper and the sleep experience, constitute everything that is here. All the three are represented by *om*. We saw that what existed earlier, what exists now and what will exist later is *om*. Everything—known-unknown, *viditam-aviditam*, including the knower—is *oṁkāraḥ*. That is the Lord, Īśvara.

When you know its meaning, *om* becomes the name of the Lord for you. Once you have said '*om*,' you will have said everything. *Om*.

Praṇava, om, is only for sannyāsins

Pure *praṇava, om,* is generally not given to *gṛhastha*s, householders. Experientially there is this conclusion that it creates *tyāga-vṛtti,* a thought of renunciation which is not appropriate for a *gṛhastha,* even though that *vṛtti* is important for a *sannyāsin*. The *praṇava* is used by *sannyāsin*s because the *gāyatrī* that was chanted before *sannyāsa* is absorbed into this *praṇava*. The *gāyatrī-mantra* and the *vyāhṛti*s, *bhūḥ*, *bhuvaḥ* and *svaḥ,* are absorbed into the *praṇava*. This is all ritually done at the time of initiation into *sannyāsa*.

Overview of Rudram and Camakam

In the *Rudram* we chant *namaste astu bhagavan viśveśvarāya... Namaḥ te astu,* Oh Lord! unto you my salutation be. Who is that Bhagavān? Viśveśvara, *viśvasya īśvaraḥ;* the Lord of the *viśva,* the entire universe. It can also be *viśvaścāsau īśvaraśca;* he is *viśva,* the universe, and he is Īśvara, the Lord. The entire *Rudram* describes Viśveśvara. In fact, the *Rudram* offers salutations unto the Lord who is in the form of the universe, *viśva,* as the one who is the giver of results for our actions, both desirable and undesirable. To gain desirable and avoid undesirable we propitiate him. Every form that we can think of, is presented as Parameśvara in the *Rudram* and we offer our salutations unto him. We surrender unto him and it is his job to take care.

In Camakam we ask the Lord to give us everything

The *Camakam* typically follows the *Rudram*. In the *Rudram,* you offer your salutation, *namaḥ*. In the *Camakam,* however, you are asking for something; '*me*' is 'to me'. The *Camakam* is a prayer asking the Lord to give you specific blessings and things. After all, as an individual you are always helpless, your efforts are inadequate and the factors over which you have no control are too numerous.

You make all your efforts, but there is still a distance you have to cover to make your efforts successful. If it is purely the problem of a living organism, the problem can somehow be addressed. Even the amoeba lives in your stomach safely. But as a human being the ambitions are too many and the resources too limited. The ambitious human being requires some help and therefore prays to the Lord. One demands a lot of things. Suppose Bhagavān were to appear in front of you and ask what you want, you simply chant the *Camakam*! Present your request to him in his own words because it includes everything. It takes care of your physical needs, it takes care of your emotional needs and it takes care of your economic needs. However, it invokes or reflects an entirely different attitude on your part; it is not an attitude of surrender.

Why should you chant the *Rudram* and subsequently ask Bhagavān for various things by chanting the *Camakam*? If you were to chant only the *Camakam*, it may be meaningful as a simple prayer. It appears incongruous that in the *Rudram* you give yourself up, and in the *Camakam* you ask him for everything. Why would you need to ask for anything if you have already surrendered to him? This incongruity can perhaps be explained if you look at the word '*me*' a little differently.

The Lord is the order that sustains everything

In the *Rudram* you have said *namaḥ* in so many words, unto the Lord who is everything and pervades the body-mind-sense complex. He is the *antaryāmin*, the inner sustainer or regulator. As Hiraṇyagarbha, the one who is the *prāṇa* in all, *antare tiṣṭhan yamayati*, abiding within, he regulates or guides. Being the nature of the 'innermost' or truth of the self, he abides within, sustaining and guiding the mind and so on, *pratyag-ātma-svarūpeṇa tiṣṭhan antaḥkaraṇādīn yamayati*. Similarly, he also sustains everything as the *vastu*, existence and consciousness, *sattā-sphūrti-pradānena sarvaṁ yamayati*. Īśvara is the *antaryāmin* of all the elements: He is the earth, *pṛthivī*; the sun, *āditya*; the air, *vāyu*, and so on. For instance, *vāyu* does not know and it does not objectify Īśvara. But as its *antaryāmin*, Īśvara provides the air, *sattā*, existence. He also regulates, *yamayati*, in sustaining and making *vāyu* perform all the functions.

Once you come to Īśvara, you cannot talk about existence and consciousness, *sattā-sphūrti*, alone. You have to bring in *māyā*. You may call it *māyā* or magic, but still there is an inherent order there. *Māyā* has a methodical manifestation, certain kind of predictability. There is bondage, *bandha*, and there is release, *mokṣa*, from that bondage in the wake of knowledge.

Until then there is *karma* and there is *karmaphala*, both the seen result, *dṛṣṭa-phala*, and the unseen, *adṛṣṭa-phala*. We learn about *dṛṣṭa-phala* from our own experiences and we learn about *adṛṣṭa-phala* from the *śāstra*. Therefore, we understand that there is an order.

Recognising the order helps reduce our subjectivity

In all our knowledge there is an element of subjectivity. The progress of knowledge is the reduction of subjectivity. When there is less subjectivity, there is more fidelity to the order and there is more Īśvara. The more we are in touch with the order, the more we are in touch with Īśvara. The complete reduction of subjectivity is possible only when we acknowledge the fact that we lack objectivity. There is no other way of eliminating subjectivity. How else is the human being with all his anxieties, fears and ambitions going to reduce all his subjectivity? It is just not possible.

We do not understand what others say because of our subjectivity. We mistake people all the time. In communication, there is so much subjectivity. For example, words like God, religion, and divinity mean different things to different people. There is subjectivity in every judgement we make about a person. Our life of ambition implies a life of aggressiveness, which is bound to make us subjective and judgemental. Therefore, we all have our permanent 'armor'. Even a smile, or a 'Hi' are different armors! How are we going to be non-judgemental? This is our life in this world, no matter where we go.

Our subjectivity is part of the order

I can acknowledge that I have subjectivity, and that subjectivity is part of the same order. Coming as I do from a background of my own, naturally, my subjectivity is logical. I cannot understand why I have this kind of subjectivity. Each person has his or her own background providing all the reasons one needs. Only Īśvara can understand all this subjectivity! The Lord pervades me as the *māyāvin*. He methodically manifests in my body, my mind, my health, my *prāṇa*, and my anatomy. Each one of us has an unconscious that has a certain uncanny logic. All this is nothing but order within. There is order outside also.

Seeing the Lord as the inner regulator, *antaryāmin*, who sustains everything merely as the existence and consciousness, is seeing the *svarūpa* of Bhagavān. That is the truth of Bhagavān, *bhagavat svarūpa*. This is entirely different from recognising Īśvara as order, sustaining the entire *jagat*.

Chanting Rudram reduces our subjectivity

I have difficulty in seeing the world as it is. More the ambition, more is the anxiety. More the anxiety, greater is the problem. This is an endless process. Therefore, to reduce the subjectivity, I say *namaḥ*. I cannot do anything else. There is no other way. This *śaraṇāgati-tattva,* the reality of surrender, has a place in the scheme of things. Therefore, I have to resign to Īśvara. My understanding is also a part of the prayer.

Offering a *patra,* leaf, and a *puṣpa,* flower, is enough only when my *bhakti* is complete. *Bhakti* cannot be complete when I have a vague idea of some higher power. That will be a vague prayer and there will be a vague result. The salutation is not understood and the Lord is not understood because I cannot put my heart and soul into it. We get only as much grace, as we are able to tap. Therefore, there is no question of my getting the maximum benefit when I am not fully involved in the prayer. The right attitude will perhaps, only, develop slowly. The *Rudram* tells that everything is Īśvara. If I have that level of understanding, the ego is already well-informed, and that *namaḥ* is complete; I have understood that every aspect of this *jagat* is his manifestation. Therefore, all that I have is the understanding of Īśvara. It is that knowledge, which consumes the ego. In fact, Īśvara has already consumed the ego, and it was my ignorance that kept mes away from Īśvara.

The vision of oneness

The better I understand the *Rudram*, the more I appreciate Īśvara. There should be that degree of clarity wherein I am totally consumed by Īśvara. This is *jñāna*. To the extent I know, to that extent I am free from subjectivity. My subjectivity is not totally removed, but if I am able to see that it is part of the order that is Īśvara, I have no problem. If that also is in accordance with the order, I am free. By the time I complete the *Rudram*, and understand, I can then recite the *Camakam*. It is all my reality, *mama-svarūpam*. Here, the word, '*me*' is taken as *mama*, my, in the genitive case. First, I surrender to Īśvara, then by his own grace I discover Īśvara to see that all that is there is me. Everything is my form, *mama-rūpāṇi*. "*Īśāvāsyam idaṁ sarvam*, everything is pervaded by the Lord."[16] That everything is the Lord can be seen to reflect my reality, *mama saccidānanda-ātmanaḥ idaṁ sarvam*, everything here is me. This reality has its being in the self, which is limitless existence, consciousness, *saccidānanda ātman.* We have to say that. Otherwise, it is incomplete. This is the *sarvātma-bhāva*, the vision of oneness. When the salutation is total, there is *sarvātma-bhāva*. When you say Īśvara is everything,

---

[16] *Īśāvasyopaniṣad* 1

you should be able to say, 'I am everything.' Only then is your understanding real, only then is it complete.

Rudram and Camakam are complementary

The *Rudram* and the *Camakam* go together. The *Camakam* says, "Everything is mine, *mama idaṁ sarvam*." But the genitive case is not used in the possessive sense. Rather, it indicates, *mama abhivyaktiḥ eva idaṁ sarvam*—all this is but my manifestation. We can use any form of declension for *ātman*, and we do see the *śāstra* doing this. For instance, there is, '*mayā tatam idaṁ sarvam*, all this is pervaded by me,' '*mama eva idaṁ sarvam*, all this is mine alone,' and '*aham eva idaṁ sarvam*, I alone am all this.' The use of any *vibhakti* is fine for every declension is nothing but Bhagavān!

In the Lord's vision everything is in order

I am sometimes asked, "Swamiji, is it right for us to ask the Lord for what we want? Does he not know what I want?" It is not his decision that makes things happen for you. It is your invoking him for certain things; you have to be very clear. Therefore, it is better that you ask him. That is why we have these specific prayers as well as broad-spectrum prayers. We have highly sophisticated forms of prayer because of our understanding of Īśvara.

The Lord is everything; he is beyond good and evil, *dharma* and *adharma*. Naciketas knew it and asked for that which is beyond *dharma* and *adharma*.

अन्यत्र धर्मादन्यत्राधर्मादन्यत्रास्मात्कृताकृतात् ।
अन्यत्र भूताच्च भव्याच्च यत्तत्पश्यसि तद्वद ॥

anyatra dharmād anyatrādharmād anyatrāsmāt kṛtākṛtāt,
anyatra bhūtācca bhavyācca yat tat paśyasi tad vada.

Please tell me of that which you see as different from *dharma* and *adharma*, different from this cause and effect, and different from the past and the future (*Kaṭhopaniṣad* 1-2-14).

Śrī Śaṅkara quotes this to prove how the *vastu* is beyond *dharma* and *adharma*. Is it not, after all, Naciketas's question? Lord Yama confirms this *vākya* in his reply. The *vākya* of Naciketas becomes a *veda-vākya* because Lord Yama confirms it. What is it which transcends *dharma* and *adharma*? "... even though I am its author, know me to be a non-doer, ever changeless."[17] It is the only resolution and the point where all opposites resolve. That is where the highest form of sanity is. Everything that operates

---

[17] "...*tasya kartāram api māṁ viddhyakartṛramavyayam*" (*Bhagavad Gītā* 4-13) .

elsewhere is instinct; it is insanity in different forms. There is sanity only when you are able to embrace both opposites and still say that you are neither of them. You can say, 'All this is I, and yet I am free from all of it.'

The Gist of Puruṣa Sūktam

The *Puruṣa Sūktam* is a popular Vedic hymn, being used often in rituals. This *sūktam* is found in all the four Vedas with minor variations. The presiding deity, the *prasiddha-puruṣa* of this *mantra* is the *paramātman.* The *ṛṣi* is Nārāyaṇa. Both the *anuṣṭubh* and the *triṣṭubh* metres are used in this *sūktam.*

Description of the puruṣa

The following two *mantra*s from the *Kaṭhopaniṣad,* talk about that which is the subtlest and the truth of everything:

इन्द्रियेभ्यः परा ह्यर्था अर्थेभ्यश्च परं मनः।
मनसस्तु परा बुद्धिर्बुद्धेरात्मा महान्परः॥

indriyebhyaḥ parā hyarthā arthebhyaśca paraṁ manaḥ, manasastu parā buddhirbuddherātmā mahānparaḥ.

महतः परमव्यक्तमव्यक्तात्पुरुषः परः।
पुरुषान्न परं किञ्चित्सा काष्ठा सा परा गतिः॥

mahataḥ param avyaktam avyaktāt puruṣaḥ paraḥ,
puruṣānna paraṁ kiñcitsā kāṣṭhā sā parā gatiḥ.

Sense objects are superior to the sense organs. Mind is superior to the sense objects.

> Intellect is superior to the mind. Hiraṇyagarbha is superior to the intellect. The unmanifest (*avyakta*) is superior to Hiraṇyagarbha. *Puruṣa* is superior to the unmanifest. Nothing is superior to the *puruṣa*. *Puruṣa* alone is the goal, the ultimate end (*Kaṭhopaniṣad* 1-3-10, 11).

We have the sense, the sense objects of our perceptions, the mind, the intellect (*buddhi*), *mahān atmā* (Hiraṇyagarbha), the unmanifest (*avyakta*), and then the *puruṣa*. The *puruṣa* is consciousness, *caitanya*, the truth of the unmanifest. This *puruṣa* alone is the ultimate end, *sā kāṣṭhā sā parā gatiḥ*.

This *puruṣa* is presented in a hymn of praise. The *Puruṣa Sūktam* is a *sūktam* for which the *puruṣa* is the object. *Uktam* is what is said. *Sūktam* or *sūktiḥ* is that which is *su uktam*, well said. A *sūktam* is to be chanted daily, *pārāyaṇa-yogya*, as a prayer. Any *sūktam* is a prayer in praise of the Lord. Some of the Vedic prayers ask the Lord to grant us something or the other. Some others are just a description of the Lord. The *Puruṣa Sūktam* is a description of the *puruṣa*. We repeat the glory of the Lord, Parameśvara, every day by chanting this *sūktam*. In so doing, we also recognise that the *puruṣa* is the self, *ātman*. There is nothing higher than the *puruṣa*, *puruṣānna paraṁ kiñcit*. I am not separate from the *puruṣa*; I am not a separate entity. The entire knowledge of the *upaniṣad*s is contained in the *Puruṣa Sūktam*. Anything that describes the *puruṣa* properly becomes an *upadeśa*, teaching. Therefore this *sūktam* is the *upadeśa*. It is descriptive of the *puruṣa*. Naturally, the *puruṣa* has to be described as the Lord with form, *saguṇa-brahma*, as well as the Lord without form, *nirguṇa-brahma*. This is presented as the cause and the effect. The *puruṣa* cannot be described in the form of the cause, and since the effect is non-separate from the cause, the description of the effect becomes the description of the *puruṣa*.

All beings are the puruṣa

The *puruṣa* is thus described in the form of the creation, in the form of all the things that exist and in the form of the very society itself. All of humanity is nothing but the *puruṣa*. Your hands and legs are the *puruṣa's* hands and legs. Your head is the *puruṣa*'s head; there is only the *puruṣa*'s head. If the *puruṣa* is understood properly your *ahaṅkāra* and *mamakāra*— 'sense of I and mine'—will be only from a point of view.

Chanting Puruṣa Sūktam regularly neutralises the sense of ownership

If all that is here is *puruṣa*, the individual, then anyone who understands this even vaguely, has to say, "He includes me." This approach creates a sense of belonging with respect to Īśvara, the total. We seek a sense of belonging wherever we go. We feel a sense of non-belonging in certain places and tend to move away from those places, such as disco, a nightclub, or even Wall Street. One place where everyone can belong is with Īśvara. He is one person who claims you because the *bhāvanā* is that your head is pervaded by his head. In that *bhāvanā*, your sense of ownership, *mamatva*, diminishes, and the erroneous I-sense, *ahaṅkāra*, slowly goes away. This *sūktam* is a prayer repeated daily, towards that end. For a Vedantin, it is the confirmation of the *śāstra*. For the person who does not know, it is manner of praising Īśvara; the daily *pārāyaṇam* helps the person establish certain relationship with Īśvara. Therefore, it is a very popular *sūktam* like the *Rudram* or the *Śrī Sūktam*.

The *Camakam* can be viewed as a detailed account of *puruṣa*, the all. When you understand the *Puruṣa Sūktam* well, you can say that the *puruṣa* is the *ātman*, the self. Then you can say, *mama idaṁ sarvam*, "Everything belongs to me, as I am not separate from anything." Instead, asking for different things, one knows that one is *puruṣa* that is everything.

In the beginning you say, *puruṣasya idaṁ sarvam*, all this belongs to *puruṣa*. When you come to see the *puruṣa* as being the *ātman*, the self, saying *mama idaṁ sarvam*, all this belongs to me, is but a declaration that everything is I.

The word *puruṣa* has two meanings: one, the person who indwells the body-mind-sense complex—*purau uṣati iti puruṣaḥ*. This body is likened to a city, *puri*. *Uṣati* means *vasati*, indwells. Like the indivisible space is seemingly enclosed in a pot, this *ātman* is seemingly enclosed in a body-mind-sense complex. However, the enclosure is only from the standpoint of the mind and does not result in any kind of division to the *ātman*. Space is not divided even though the pot, which is an *upādhi*, encloses the space within it. Similarly, he who is the all-pervasive, *sarvagata*, and complete, *pūrṇa*, is manifest through a given body-mind-sense complex.

The other meaning of *puruṣa* is *pūrṇatvāt puruṣaḥ*, he is the *puruṣa* because he is complete, full. The *puruṣa* is the one who fills or permeates all this, *sarvaṁ pūrayati iti puruṣaḥ*, the one who abides in this entire creation. If we repeat *puruṣaḥ* twice, we mean that he is the one who abides in the entire creation and resides in the city that is our body. This *puruṣa*, even though remaining in this body, fills up everything that is here. Repeating the word *puruṣaḥ* twice as, '*puruṣaḥ puruṣaḥ*,' we have the entire teaching, *upadeśa*. The *upadeśa* is that this individual self, the *jīva*, is Lord, who is all. Just as we have the teaching, '*tat tvam asi*, that thou art,' we have *puruṣaḥ eva puruṣaḥ*.

In the *sūkta*, *puruṣa* who is a conscious being is not presented as someone who possesses one body.

We all know the person, 'I,' very well. The one who is in this body has one body, one mind, and one set of senses, one *kārya-karaṇa-saṅghāta*, while that *puruṣa* in the hymn is all heads, all legs, all eyes. How both can be one? If the I-sense, *ahaṅkāra*, is taken as one body-mind-sense complex, we cannot understand this *vākya*, sentence. Then how is this *sūktam* to be understood? We have to step out of this level of identification and go to the *ahaṅkāra-adhiṣṭhāna*, the basis for the ego, the *sākṣī*, the witness. From there, look at the entire physical universe from the point of view of the consciousness which is the self, the *caitanya-ātman*. All of it, including space, *ākāśa*, air, *vāyu*, fire, *agni*, waters, *ap*, and earth, *pṛthivī*, is born of this *puruṣa* alone and is non-separate from this *puruṣa*.

Does this *puruṣa* have only one physical body-mind-sense complex? No. He is every body-mind-sense complex. Everything belongs to him alone. Then how many *śīrṣa*s, heads has he? He has countless heads! The word *sahasra* does not mean a countable number; it means countless. Some, mistakenly, take this literally as meaning a thousand heads, thousand eyes and so on. It is a word that implies more than what is expressed, an *upalakṣaṇa*. This is the Lord as the whole cosmos, *virāṭ-svarūpa*. *Vividhaṁ rājate iti virāṭ*, the one who appears in this manifold form is the *virāṭ-puruṣa*. This *puruṣa* has countless heads;

he is *sahasrākṣa*, has countless eyes. He is *sahasrapāt*, all the feet are his feet.

Sa bhūmiṁ viśvato vṛtvā. *Bhūmi* is not only the earth, but the spherical form of the cosmos, *brahmāṇḍa-golaka-rūpam*. We have always looked upon the earth as being a sphere, *golaka*, and not as being flat. *Vṛtvā* means *vyāpya*, pervading. The *puruṣa* encloses all of it, permeating, pervading everything, *viśvataḥ*, without exception, without omitting any place.

The Lord can be recognised in the heart

Atyatiṣṭhad daśāṅgulam is *daśāṅgulam ati-atiṣṭhat*. You can ascribe two meanings to *daśāṅgulam*. One is that he is apart from you by ten inches, or stands ten inches away. The space of ten inches indicates that he stands unaffected. While pervading everything, he is yet far away from everything. He is both *saguṇaṁ brahma* and *nirguṇaṁ brahma*. Why the term *daśāṅgulam*? It is just a figurative expression, an *upalakṣaṇa*. It means he is miles away. Then why not say miles away? This is because he is so very close by! Ten inches is very close. He is very close to you and yet he is far away from you. He himself is everything, and still, he transcends everything.

Daśāṅgulam also symbolises the place in the heart, *hṛdaya-sthāna*. He is the one who stays close, pervading everything in your heart, the *daśāṅgula-hṛdaya*.

You could also understand it to mean that he pervades everything, as the *para-ātman*, even while abiding right in your heart. That is the place where he can be recognised, his *upalabdhi-sthānam*. The *hṛdaya* stands for the intellect, *buddhi*. He presides over the *buddhi* as the *jñātṛ*, knower, as *jñāna*, knowledge, and the *jñeya*, object to be known. This is the other meaning of *daśāṅgulam*.

The Lord is everything

Puruṣa evedaguṁ sarvam—puruṣaḥ eva idaṁ sarvam, *puruṣa* alone is all this. A lot of people commit mistakes in interpreting the *Puruṣa Sūktam*. One problematic translation is that from the mouth of that *puruṣa* came the priestly class, the *brāhmaṇa*, from the hands came the warriors, the *kṣatriya*, from the *ūru*, the navel, came the traders, the *vaiśya*, and from the feet, the working class, *śūdra*. So in defense of the *śūdra*s, they claim that they are in no way inferior in spite of having come from the feet of the *puruṣa*. "Without the feet and legs there is no *puruṣa*. There is no society without the *śūdra*s, the working class. What would happen to the other classes if the working class were not there? Therefore, the working class is very important. The legs of Bhagavān are more important than the head of Bhagavān!"

What is the "*idaṁ sarvam*–all this"? The section in question says, "The *brāhmaṇa* was his face," *brāhmaṇaḥ asya mukham asīt*, and not "from his face was the *brāhmaṇa,*" *asya mukhāt brāhmaṇaḥ asīt.* All of humanity is his form. Why? As we saw, he has countless eyes, countless feet and pervades the entire cosmos without exception, *sahasrākṣaḥ sahasrapāt sa bhūmiṁ viśvato vṛtvā.* In fact. the *Puruṣa Sūktam* asks itself some questions—What are his hands, what are his legs, what is his face, and so on? Then it says that the face, *mukha,* is the *brāhmaṇa,* the feet are the *sūdra,* etc. In fact, he is everything, *idaṁ sarvam.*

He is the lord of time and of all the worlds

Yadbhūtaṁ yacca bhavyam. The entire cosmos, *brahmāṇḍa,* including the 14 worlds, *loka*s, are this *puruṣa* alone, *idaṁ sarvaṁ puruṣaḥ eva.* He is there even in the worlds of the Gods, *devaloka*s. Each *loka* has a presiding deity, an *adhiṣṭhāna-devatā.* Like Indra is the presiding *devatā* of heaven, *svarga,* and Brahmāji, of *brahmaloka,* he is the *swāmi* of all the *devatā*s who preside over other *loka*s.

Yadannenātirohati. Yad stands for the *puruṣa. Annena atirohati,* he is manifest in different forms of enjoyment, *bhoga,* for all the *jīva*s, giving up his earlier unmanifest state, but without ever giving up his true nature, *svarūpa.* This manifest form is an incidental *kārya* or effect, and therefore, not the *svarūpa.* An effect, *kārya,* is always *mithyā.* He has assumed this form and, therefore, remains in the heart.

Introduction to Viṣṇusahasranāma

Why so many names?

The *Viṣṇusahasranāma* is a compilation of the different names of the Lord. Why should I chant all these names? Can I not repeat any one name several times? If there are so many Viṣṇus, which one am I calling? The word Viṣṇu is applicable only to the Lord. It is derived from the root *viṣḷ, vyāptau,* meaning to pervade. So Viṣṇu means one who is all-pervasive. The all-pervasive is only one, not more than one. This name is appropriate only for the Lord, and nobody else. Therefore, when I call out to Viṣṇu, nobody else but the Lord can come. Being all-pervasive, he cannot be away from me; he is inside as well as outside. The moment I call for Viṣṇu, there is no question of him not hearing me. Why, then, are there so many names? If he does not respond to one name, will he respond to a different one? These verses are not even complete sentences that I can understand through syntax.

The names of the Lord in the *Viṣṇusahasranāma* are so many words, one after another. The reason there are so many names is that if you do not understand one word, you can go on to the next. If you do not understand the second word, there is the third, and so on. The *Amarakośa*, authored by Amarasimha, is the classic Sanskrit thesaurus.

Unlike a dictionary, this consists only of a series of synonyms and not meanings or explanations. For instance, when we look up the word Viṣṇu,[18] it says Kṛṣṇa, Dāmodara, and so on. However, if you do not understand any of the 1000 words, what do you do? Then you need to understand them.

"But, I am praising the Lord by chanting the *sahasranāma*." Who are you to praise the Lord? You can praise a person only when you are an equal, that is, when you have adequate knowledge to understand who the person is. You cannot flatter Īśvara. You flatter someone only when you describe the person as being greater than he is. In fact, when you cannot describe the Lord adequately to begin with, how can you presume to say something that describes him as being greater than he is? For example, let us analyse the praise, "Oh Lord! You are omniscient, all-knowledge." You cannot call him all-knowledge because you yourself do not know what it means. It is like Einstein being praised as the greatest scientist of his time by an elementary school dropout! Einstein would be neither flattered nor praised by his words.

As an individual, *jīva*, I must be qualified to praise the Lord. If the Lord is all-knowledge, I have no way of understanding what all-knowledge is. I have

---

18 ... *dāmadaro hṛṣīkeśaḥ keśavo mādhavaḥ svabhūḥ* (*Amarakośa* 1.1.38)

limited knowledge and cannot even spell the word omniscient. If he is a Bhagavān of infinite virtues, where is the question of praising or flattering him?

A stotra is meaningful only when it comes from a wise person

Suppose one commits to writing an *aṣṭottaraśata-nāmāvali,* a set of 108 names, one may, at some point, run out of meaningful names to write, but would need to keep on writing names nevertheless. We do find such meaningless names in some of the *aṣṭottaraśata-nāmāvali*s. We still use them because, for Bhagavān everything is okay. The author is very important in such *stotra*s because we are talking of the Lord. The words have to come from a heart that knows. It is a set of words coming from somebody who understands his or her own limitations, and at the same time understands the Lord because of the *śāstra*. That is why the *śāstra* is so important here.

The *stotra* is meaningful only when it comes from one who knows the *śāstra*. The human mind cannot fathom Īśvara, but the *śāstra* is something that we can employ to understand Īśvara and bless ourselves. Generally, our knowledge is fraught with ignorance; we may know something in one area, but not know much in many others. Even to ask questions in a particular area, we need to know many things about it. We do not know enough even to ask questions. Therefore, who is this human being to praise the Lord?

Those who understand the *śāstra* may not know what all-knowledge means, but they do know that the word 'omniscient' describes one who is free from ignorance and confusion. The one who praises the Lord is the one who is 'I know' and 'I don't know' person. If the 'I know' statement is more and the 'I don't know' is less, you are almost all-knowing. However, our situation is such that 'I don't know' is always much more than 'I know'. The area of ignorance is not there in the one who is all-knowledge which is why you can use the wonderful word *ananta* to describe the Lord at every level. He is *ananta* in terms of time, *ananta* in terms of space, and *ananta* in terms of knowledge, wisdom, and creativity. You can understand and address Īśvara this way and it would not be mere praise at all.

However, if the praise, *praśaṁsā*, comes from the heart of one who knows, those words become meaningful. Veda Vyāsa is such a person. He is a *sarvajña-kalpa*, one who has knowledge in all the areas that count, that makes life meaningful. From Veda Vyāsa have come these names forming what is known as *Viṣṇusahasranāma*. These names are not ordinary words. They are highly meaningful. Many names of the Lord in the *Viṣṇusahasranāma* reveal the nature of Bhagavān. If you understand their meaning, you will find that the names contain the essence of Vedanta.

A word and its meaning are inseparable

A word, *vāk*, and its meaning, *artha*, are inseparable. Once you know the meaning of a word, it is never separate from the word in your mind. Until then, a word is just a sound or set of sounds. Therefore, a word is a word only when you know its meaning. Once the meaning is known, the word disappears giving way to its meaning. Only the meaning remains in your mind as an object of recognition. That is what we mean when we say a word and its meaning are inseparable.

Words can be meaningful only when they come from somebody who knows the *śāstra*, a *śāstrajña*. Only a *śāstrajña* can write. Coming as they do from a heart that really understands Īśvara, words become an expression of *bhakti*, an expression of that person's knowledge of Īśvara. Through these words we get in touch with the devotion in the heart of that person. We also arrive at the vision of Īśvara, the truth of Īśvara. This is the reason why we have *stotra*s like the *Viṣṇusahasranāma*.

There are *sahasranāma*s of different deities, but many of the names are the same in form or in meaning. Only the words that describe the episodes, *līlā*s, in the various incarnations of the Lord will be different. Since that truth is only one, the words are bound to be the same in form or in their meaning. Bhagavān Vyāsa is arguably the most important link in the Vedic tradition. This *sahasranāma* is presented by the sage in his astounding epic, *Mahābhārata*.

Īśvara is revealed by the One Thousand Names in the *Viṣṇusahasranāma*. The more you understand the words, the less alienated you are from Īśvara. Once this is understood, the repetition of these words becomes a means of contemplation. I know many learned *mahātmā*s daily repeating these words, and 'seeing' their meaning. More often than not, they are bound to be the very meaning of these words. This is called *nididhyāsana*, contemplation, necessary for abiding *niṣṭhā*.

Three sets of words

Svarūpa names

All the *sahasranāma*s comprise three groups of words. One group of words reveals the *svarūpa* of Īśvara, which is one, non-dual. Whether you read the *sahasranāma* of Śiva, Viṣṇu, or Devī, these words are similar. For example, in describing the *svarūpa* of the Lord, the name *ānanda* will be used, *ānanda-svarūpāya namaḥ* or *ānandasvarūpiṇyai namaḥ*. The only difference is that where Īśvara is invoked as a Goddess, the words that reveal the truth of Īśvara are in the feminine gender.

Each of these words revealing the *svarūpa* is Vedanta and has to be understood in the context of the entire *vedānta-śāstra*. Without adequate teaching of Vedanta only a vague idea one can get but that is enough for making the recitation as a rewarding prayer. When we have understood the *śāstra*, we would be the *svarūpa* as we recite this *stotra*.

Guṇa names

There is another group of words in *sahasranāma*s which describe the *guṇa*s, the glories of Īśvara, such as *sarva-kaṛtre namaḥ, sṛṣṭi-kartre namaḥ*, the one who has created this world, and is manifest in the form of the world. *Guṇa* names help us relate to Īśvara. From this standpoint we can see Īśvara as the one who sustains everything, and the one unto whom everything goes back. Words like *sarvavyāpin*, one who pervades everything, *sarvajña*, one who knows everything, are not the *svarūpa* of Īśvara, but the *guṇa*s of Īśvara with reference to the entire *jagat*. These words can convey that Īśvara is one who is in the form of sun, space, earth, fire, and so on. They can also be found saying that he is the brilliance of the brilliant, the heat of the fire, and so on, depicting the glories.

There are words describing him as one who is all compassion, *dayā-svarūpa*, whose form is one of blessing, *maṅgala-vigraha*. We do have all these qualities in small measure, but Īśvara has these in infinite measure. These are called *kalyāṇa-guṇa*s of the Lord. In repeating these words, we invoke in ourselves what we see in Īśvara, and thus we do imbibe them. This is simple psychology; we pick up what we love and appreciate in someone we look up to. For example, if you admire a teacher's handwriting, you are likely to pick up his or her handwriting. When you are devoted to an altar, you admire, praise and invoke these qualities in the altar; you imbibe them as a rule.

When you admire Īśvara as one who is everything that you have, one who is everything that there is, your *ahaṅkāra*, the false unenlightened ego, is objective. You require your heavy ego to be lightened before you are enlightened.

Enlightenment is understanding the *svarūpa* of the Lord. For that, you have to bring in more Īśvara into your life. Saying, "Let Go, Let God," is not enough, even though helpful. Only in clarity can you relax, not in vagueness. Even when facing a problem, if you have clarity about the problem, you are sure how to go about it. Clarity does not come from the heavens or even by pushing yourself into some corner. Clarity comes from keeping yourself in a certain prayerful inner and external atmosphere of learning. That amounts to saying, "seek *satsaṅga* with a prayerful heart and open mind."

Līlā names

The third set of words reveals how Īśvara actively participates in answering the devotee's prayers. No prayer goes unanswered. A prayerful person always benefits from his or her prayers. In order to convey this message, we have the *līlā-vigraha* of Parameśvara, the Lord in various *avatāras*, as Kṛṣṇa, as Rāmā, as Narasiṁha. In all these *avatāras*, one thing is to be understood. The Lord answers the prayers of devotees even if it amounts to assuming a certain form, whether human or non-human, to accomplish a certain end. Even when he assumes a human form to live along with other humans, he stands out as always being there for one to look up to, as one who can help. *Līlā* names assure the devotee that their prayers will be answered

What is strikingly clear to a human being is his or her helplessness in situations. To know that there is help that one can seek, is a relief. That I can help myself is a good assumption to begin with. I would like to help myself as far as I can because I am given two hands, I am given a scheme of things, I am given a certain set of skills, I am given the capacity to hone my skills, and I am given a faculty to know. That I already know a few things, and can know a few other things so that I can help myself, is perfect. Even so, I can help myself only up to an extent.

I always find myself in a corner from where I cannot move any further in terms of knowledge, skill, and power. This is called helplessness, *dainya, dīnasya bhāvaḥ dainyam.* That is why when anybody talks about *dainya,* everybody begins to empathise naturally because everyone goes through it. We can easily identify with the prayer line: "You are Prabhu, the Lord, but I am helpless." Actually, it is not that I am entirely helpless. I can peel a banana; yes. But even that is not possible for one if there is paralysis.

As far as I can help myself I do help myself, and beyond that, I seek help. There are others, whom I can look up to, seek help from. I can tap other sources. Nevertheless, I can be prayerful all the way because that is the attitude in keeping with the reality of living. The hidden variables are too numerous as even my ambitions and desires. Therefore, human effort should include prayer, to control the hidden as well as tough situations very well known.

Invoke the Lord's grace through prayer

One needs to invoke the grace that makes a difference between success and failure. That grace needs to be there all the way. One breathes in, hoping that one will breathe out, and one breathes out hoping that one will breathe in. There is a time when one breathes one's last. That possibility is always there. Therefore, when somebody asks me where grace is, I answer that the grace is between two heartbeats, between 'lub' and 'dub'. This is how it goes: lub, grace, dub, grace, lub, grace, dub, grace and so on.

One needs to recognise intimately, the limitation of oneself in terms of one's knowledge, skill, resources, strength and capacities. Whichever way one looks at oneself, the limitation is strikingly obvious. One can say, "I am limited," and droop or one can still walk erect, with a prayerful attitude, doing as much as one can.

Seek help from one who does not need help

We discover through the stories from the *purāṇa*s that Īśvara listens to our entreaties. Īśvara has gained a few names as the one who answered prayers, as the one who is available as a source of help. We have to seek help from a source that is available. Everybody around us is equally helpless and seeking help. Even a doctor who administers medicine needs help. The doctor gives us medicine with a prayer because he or she knows the contra-indications! We seek each other's help all the time, but all are equally needy of grace which is why we have to go to Bhagavān. The words indicating the *līla* present the Lord as one who actively participates in the lives of individuals in response to their prayer. In the *purāṇas*, we have the account of the various *avatāras*. Some of the words in the *sahasranāma* are culled from these *avatāras*.

We have these three sets of words in every *sahasranāma*. One is the depiction of the *svarūpa* of Parameśvara. The other describes Parameśvara manifesting in the form of this great *jagat*, having infinite qualities. Then we have Parameśvara who appears in response to the prayer of his *bhaktas*. The forms that he assumes to protect *dharma*, *dharma-saṁsthāpana*, give rise to the third set of words.

Pūrṇa-kumbha mantra

The four verses of the *pūrṇa-kumbha-mantra*, from *na karmaṇā na prajayā* to *yaḥ paraḥ saḥ maheśvaraḥ,* are typically chanted when receiving *sannyāsins*. Originally, the *pūrṇa-kumbha-mantra* used to begin with the chanting of an additional section, *yo devānaṁ prathamaṁ purastād,* followed by these four *mantras*. Together, these *mantras* are called the *Ācārya-pañcādi*.

न कर्मणा न प्रजया धनेन
त्यागेनैके अमृतत्वमानशुः ।
परेण नाकं निहितं गुहायां
विभ्राजते यद्यतयो विशन्ति ॥

na karmaṇā na prajayā dhanena tyāgenaike
amṛtatvamānaśuḥ, pareṇa nākaṁ
nihitaṁ guhāyāṁ vibhrājate yadyatayo viśanti.

Not by work, nor by progeny or by wealth, but by renunciation alone have some attained immortality. That (immortality) which is even beyond the heaven, is attained by the self-controlled renunciates (as the Self) shining in their heart.

Amṛtatvam ānaśuḥ, amṛtatvam ānaśire prāptavantaḥ, these people have gained immortality or freedom from death, *mokṣa*. They have gained freedom from *saṁsāra*. *Saṁsarati* iti *saṁsāraḥ*. *Saṁsāra* is a life that is subject to change, e.g., *ahaṁ sukhī*, I am happy or *ahaṁ duḥkhī*, I am unhappy. Freedom from *saṁsāra* is *amṛtatva*. So *amṛtatva* means *mokṣa*, freedom from time, freedom from death.

Who are they who gain this *amṛtatva*? *Tyāginaḥ*. *Tyāgena eke prāptavantaḥ*, by renunciation some gain. *Eke* in the plural means a few people. By what means? *Tyāgena*, by *tyāga*. *Tyāga* is renunciation for the sake of knowledge. These are *sannyāsins* who have renounced to gain knowledge, to gain *mokṣa*. *Sannyāsa* is praised in this *mantra*. The *mantra* will explain this further.

Na karmaṇā, not by *karma*. One can gain *mokṣa* only by knowledge. *Karma* will bring *karmaphala*, results, but *karma* is finite and therefore, *karmaphala* is also finite. The limited person plus the limited result born of limited *karma* will continue to be limited. A finite number when added to a finite number will still be a finite number. Therefore, *na karmaṇā*, there is no way of getting *mokṣa* through *karma*.

Can *karma-yoga* lead to *mokṣa*? Yes, you can gain knowledge by *karma-yoga*, in that it prepares you for knowledge. It is not just another form of *yoga*. We mistakenly think that we will perform *karma-yoga*.

Nobody can 'do' *karma-yoga*. There is no particular action called *karma-yoga*. Some people believe that in giving as charity or in doing some *sevā*, they are 'doing' *karma-yoga*. *Karma-yoga* is only possible when your goal is *mokṣa*, and the entire life is one of proper attitude. For instance, your conduct and duties in marriage or parenting are also part of *karma-yoga*. You can thus convert your activities in life into a means for your own growth; that is *karma-yoga*.

Na prajayā, not by progeny. *Na dhanena,* not by wealth. There are predominant desires such as the desire for wealth, fame, and power in this world, and the desire for the heavens, etc. *Puṇya-karma* is *dharma*, *dhana* is *artha*, and *prajā* is *kāma*. *Dharmārtha-kāma* is not *mokṣa*. You have to deliberately choose *mokṣa*. *Dharma* is useful in that it becomes a basis for conducting your life, and then the whole life becomes *yoga*.

Paramānanda is attained by renunciation

Tyāgenaike amṛtatvamānaśuḥ. Only by *tyāga,* renunciation of *karma,* can you gain *mokṣa*. Not doing *karma* is not renunciation. Even while performing *karma,* you should discover that you are actionless.[19] That is *akarma*. You can gain *mokṣa* only by knowing that the *ātman* is *akartṛ* and that it is Brahman.

---

[19] *Karmaṇyakarma yaḥ paśyet*… (*Bhagavad Gītā* 4-18)

Pareṇa nākam. Kam means happiness, *su-kham*. Even without the prefix '*su*,' *kham* means happiness. *Akam* is *na sukham,* that is *duḥkham. Na akam* is the absence of *duḥkha. Akaṁ na vidyate yasmin tad nākam,* that in which there is no *duḥkha* is *nākam. Nākam* is the *sukha* of heaven, which is mentioned in the Vedas. It is *anitya,* lasting only for a finite period. *Pareṇa nākam* means more than the heavenly *sukha*. It is *ānanda,* limitless. It transcends *svarga*; it transcends the absence of *duḥkha* and is in the form of *ānanda,* untouched or uninhibited by *duḥkha*. It is *paramānanda*.

Ignorance veils the Lord's presence in the intellect

Guhāyāṁ nihitam–that which obtains as yourself, the *ātman* in your *buddhi-guhā. Guhā* means cave. By definition, *guhā* is dark; it stands for darkness. The Lord obtains in the *buddhi* in the form of *ānanda,* limitlessness or fullness, as the *svarūpa* or very nature of the *ātman*. However, you do not recognise it due to ignorance. Its presence is hidden for want of light. Therefore, the faculty of knowledge, the *buddhi,* is called *guhā*.

Brahman is not hidden because everything is Brahman. The knower is Brahman, the knowledge is Brahman, and the known is Brahman. Every thought is Brahman; nothing is outside Brahman. Therefore, Brahman cannot be hidden by anything. One of the

Upaniṣad says that if a person could cover space with a cloth, he would cover Brahman! This means all that is here is Brahman. Even while you say, "I don't know Brahman," it is Brahman that is talking to me. It is as self-contradictory as saying, "I have no tongue," or "I am dead." This is denial of Brahman. You cannot deny Brahman because you are Brahman. If everything is Brahman, how is it that you do not appreciate this fact? This is because it is a question of knowing it, and not a question of believing so. This knowledge is not hidden, but veiled due to ignorance and therefore, the *buddhi* is called *guhā*.

The *buddhi* is dark with respect to Brahman, the most obvious. If you have not seen an object, it is out of sight and, therefore, out of mind, but Brahman, being oneself, is never out of sight; it never goes out of mind. Therefore, it is our ignorance that conceals its presence.

Yad vibhrājate, that which shines. It is that which shines in the form of *ānanda*, the *ātman*, consciousness. *Vividhaṁ bhrājate,* or *viśeṣeṇa bhrājate.* In the form of this entire *jagat,* that *ānanda* alone is shining all the time on the platform of one's *buddhi* as *jñātṛ-jñāna-jñeya,* the knower, knowledge and the known. Otherwise, how does one recognise any thing? Everything is in the *buddhi.* All these galaxies 'out there' are 'in here' within our *buddhi.*

The sannyāsins committed to knowledge 'gain' paramānanda

Yatayaḥ viśanti. Yatayaḥ is the plural form of *yatiḥ*. A *yati* is *yatna-śīlaḥ,* one who puts in the right effort. This can mean anybody. Even a *karma-yogin* is a *yati. Yati* also means seeker, a *mumukṣu*. The *rūḍi,* conventional meaning of *yati,* however, is *sannyāsin*. This meaning is more popular. The effort of these *yatayaḥ, sannyāsins* or *mumukṣus,* is made for the sake of *mokṣa, mokṣārthaṁ yatnam.*

Viśanti, labhante, they gain. *Yad vibhrājate tat yatayaḥ viśanti,* the *sannyāsins* attain this shining, pure *ānanda.*

How do they gain this knowledge?

वेदान्तविज्ञानसुनिश्चितार्थाः
सन्यासयोगाद्यतयः शुद्धसत्त्वाः ।
ते ब्रह्मलोके तु परान्तकाले
परामृतात् परिमुच्यन्ति सर्वे ॥

vedāntavijñānasuniścitārthāḥ
sanyāsayogādyatayaḥ śuddhasattvāḥ,
te brahmaloke tu parāntakāle
parāmṛtāt parimucyanti sarve.

> Those who make proper effort and whose minds are pure, who have well-ascertained, clear knowledge of Vedanta, because of a life of *sannyāsa*, they, at the time of the resolution of the individuality in Brahman, are all released from (even) the unmanifest (*karma*).

Vedāntavijnānam. Vedānām antaḥ Vedāntaḥ, at the end of all the Vedas is Vedanta, the *upaniṣad*. What is it that is unfolded by Vedanta? It is the knowledge of I, the *ātman*, being the whole, the limitless *brahma*. All of Vedanta is contained in one sentence, '*tat tvam asi*–you are that.' There is an obvious difference between Īśvara, the Lord, and you, the individual. He is almighty and all-knowledge, whereas, you have limited might and limited knowledge. Yet, you are equated to Īśvara! The difference is obvious and therefore the equation. If the non-difference were obvious, we would not need an equation, and, if the difference were real, there would be no equation either. You need an equation only when the difference is obvious but not real. This is the knowledge which is to be gained by Vedanta.

Suniścitārthāḥ. Niścitam means ascertained, and *suniścitam* is very well-ascertained, without any doubt whatsoever. *Suniścitam artham* is *vedānta-vijñānasya artham. Tad yeṣānte, vedānta-vijñānasya arthaḥ yeṣānte.* Those who have a well-ascertained knowledge of Vedanta. They have to put all that they know to test, attacking their knowledge from different standpoints. That is when all the schools of thought fall apart. Schools of thought exist where there are opinions involved. In knowledge, there are no schools of thought.

There are two types of errors: one that needs one-time correction, and another that needs to be corrected repeatedly. The second type of error needs to be corrected again and again not because of re-appearance of ignorance, but because of a habit of taking oneself to be other than what one is. That is where the problem is. This is *viparīta-bhāvanā*, habitual error in *jñāna*. This habit could be there because of the deeply ingrained orientation that, "I am only this much." To neutralise it one requires certain kind of contemplation. That is why a life of *sannyāsa* is necessary, *sannyāsayogāt*.

Śuddhasattvāḥ are those whose minds are not assailed by *rāga-dveṣa*, likes and dislikes, because of their having lived a life of *karma-yoga*. The word *sattva* has many meanings. Anything existent is called *sattva*. It also means one of the three *guṇa*s. The third meaning is the thinking faculty that is born of the *sattva-guṇa*. *Śuddhaṁ sattvam eṣāṁ te*. *Śuddha* is clean or cleansed, *sattva* is the mind, *eṣām*, for whom, *te*, they, are called *śuddhasattvāḥ*. They live a life of *sannyāsa* which is characterised by a pursuit of knowledge to the exclusion of everything else.

Karma-yoga is the pursuit of knowledge along with *karma,* duties, etc. A *karma-yogin,* who seeks *mokṣa,* is a *mumukṣu.* If *mokṣa* is not an end in view, the person is a *karmin* or *karmaṭha.* He can be an ethical person, a *dhārmika,* whose commitment is only towards *artha-kāma* or *lokāntara,* the other worlds. He believes in *puṇya-pāpa,* and is interested in heaven. He has nothing to do with *mokṣa,* because he thinks that going to heaven is *mokṣa,* the ultimate end.

Sannyāsayogāt. Having given up the pursuits of security and the pleasures of the world, such people take to a life of *sannyāsa* for the pursuit of knowledge. Their commitment to knowledge is more important than the life-style of *sannyāsa.* By taking up this life, they are *yatayaḥ. Mokṣa* is the *prayojana,* result, of *vedāntavijñāna.* They discover the freedom in *ātman* and have no doubts whatsoever, that the *ātman* is free. The notion that it is bound and confined falls apart.

Such sannyāsins are totally liberated

Te brahmaloke tu parāntakāle parāmṛtāt parimucyanti sarve. Te sarve, all of them, *parimucyanti, paritaḥ mucyanti,* totally liberated. Not only are they totally liberated when they are alive, but they never come back after death. In death it is only the body that dies, Brahman does not die. Such people are non-separate from Īśvara and do not come back as *jīva*s. That particular *jīva* is no longer the *jīva.*

Te brahmaloke tu parāntakāle. Kāla means time. *Antakāla* means at the end of this body or at the end of one's life. For a *jīva* there is no *antakāla.* A *jīva* travels from one body to another. He is a traveler. He stays in a body for a length of time, and then goes away. The giving up of this tenement is called death, *sthūla-śarīra-bhaṅga-kāla,* when the physical body is no longer alive.

There is another *kāla* called *parāntakāla.* This is the *sūkṣma-kāraṇa-śarīra-bhaṅga-kāla,* the end of subtle and causal bodies. The *sūkṣma-śarīra,* subtle body, generally never dies; it is either in the unmanifest form, *avyakta,* or in the manifest form, *vyakta.* At the *sūkṣma-śarīra-bhaṅga-kāla,* even the subtle body and the causal body are no more there. Not only is the body gone, the *jīva* is also no more; it is resolved. Since there is no more *karma* left, the *sūkṣma-śarīra* does not linger. Thus, the *jīva*s are liberated even while living. When they give up the physical body there is no *sūkṣma-śarīra* left and they exist as Īśvara for the *jīva*s.

Brahma eva lokaḥ brahmalokaḥ. Brahman itself is the *loka,* the self because of which all experience is possible. *Lokyate anena iti lokaḥ. Loka* is the consciousness because of which you become conscious of everything. *Tasmin brahmaloke parimucyanti sarve*–in that Brahman they are all released. From what?

Parāmṛtat, that which is *para* or different even from the causal state, *amṛta.* The causal state never goes away. It manifests, then becomes unmanifest, manifests again, and again becomes unmanifest, and so on. Nothing really dies; the whole *jagat* and the *jīva* can become unmanifest, and then manifest. The unmanifest condition is called *parāmṛta. Para* means *kāraṇa,* the cause. It is *amṛta;* it does not die away.

Parāmṛta is that which is *param* as well as *amṛtam, paraṁ ca amṛtaṁ ca, parāmṛtam. Avyaktād api parimucyanti sarve,* even from the *avyakta* they are all released. *Avyakta* means all the *sañcita-karma,* which is *avyakta,* not manifest so far. They gain liberation even from that and do not come back again.

Tu is used for emphasis. The word *brahmaloka* is used to indicate that the *brahmaloka* talked about in this *mantra* is different from the other *brahmaloka,* which is better known as the abode of Brahmāji.

Another meaning of this verse is that the *yatayaḥ* go to *brahmaloka* and achieve *krama-mukti* when the cycle of Brahmāji is over, at the *antakāla* of the current Brahmāji.

दह्रं विपापं परमेश्मभूतं
यत्पुण्डरीकं पुरमध्यसꣳस्थम् ।
तत्रापि दह्रं गगनं विशोकस्-
तस्मिन् यदन्तस्तदुपासितव्यम् ॥

dahraṁ vipāpaṁ parameśmabhūtaṁ
yatpuṇḍarīkaṁ puramadhyasaṁstham,
tatrāpi dahraṁ gaganaṁ viśokas-
tasmin yadantastadupāsitavyam.

That, which abides in the city of the body, in the lotus, which is the intellect, and in that small space, that, which is free of all hurt and guilt, free from sorrow, and of the nature of Parameśvara, should be meditated upon.

Upāsitavyam, to be contemplated upon. What is it? The self which is free from *pāpa,* is *śuddha* and is *vipāpa. Pāpa-rahitam, nityaśuddham, ātmānam,* the self that is free from *pāpa* and is always pure. That self is *viśoka,* free from sadness, meaning that it is *sukha-svarūpa,* the very nature of happiness. *Viśoka* is freedom from hurt and *vipāpa* is freedom from guilt. The *ātman* that is free from hurt and guilt should be meditated upon.

Yat puṇḍarīkam. Puṇḍarīka is the *hṛdaya*, the heart. *Hṛtpuṇḍarike upāsitavyam.* The *ātman* should be meditated upon in the heart.

Puramadhye. Pura is this *deha*, a city. *Puramadhya* is the *buddhi. Puramadhye saṁstham* means *samsthitam*, or *samyak sthitam*, that which is self-existent, not dependant upon anything. This is the *ātma-tattva*, the truth of the self. It is in the *daharākāśa*, that which obtains in the *buddhi.* It is like *gagana*, space, without any distortion.

Parameśmabhūtam goes with *yatpuṇḍarīkam. Parameśma* is Parameśvara. It is the *svarūpa* of Parameśvara, and is not separate from Parameśvara.

Tasmin, in the *buddhi, yadantaḥ,* which is of this nature, *upāsitavyam,* that is to be contemplated upon.

यो वेदादौ स्वरः प्रोक्तो वेदान्ते च प्रतिष्ठितः।
तस्य प्रकृतिलीनस्य यः परः स महेश्वरः॥

yo vedādau svaraḥ prokto vedānte ca pratiṣṭhitaḥ,
tasya prakṛtilīnasya yaḥ paraḥ sa maheśvaraḥ.

The one who is the syllable (*om*) that is uttered at the beginning of the Veda and is well-established in the *upaniṣad*s, the one who is the cause, the truth of that causal principle which is resolved (in himself), he is the Lord, Maheśvara.

Svara is *om,* the single syllable. *Vedādau* means in the beginning of the Veda or before chanting the Veda. *Proktaḥ,* it is always chanted. *Vedānte ca pratiṣṭhitaḥ, pratipāditaḥ,* it is well established, unfolded, in Vedanta.

Om is *abhidhāna,* name and the *abhidheya,* what is indicated by the word, is Brahman. *Om* consists of the three letters, *a, u,* and *m.* The *a-kāra* stands for the wakeful state, the physical world, and it is *viśva* and Virāṭ. The *u-kāra* represents the experience of dream, and is *taijasa* and Hiraṇygarbha. The *ma-kāra* signifies the state of deep sleep, and is *prājña* and Īśvara. The *oṁkāra* is also that which transcends all the three periods of time.

Tasya prakṛtilīnasya. Prakṛtiḥ līnā yasmin, him, unto whom the entire *prakṛti* resolves totally. All *nāma-rūpa* being *prakṛti,* resolves entirely into the causal form, the unmanifest condition, and then emerges again.

Yaḥ paraḥ sa maheśvaraḥ. Yaḥ paraḥ, that is the *paraḥ. Prakṛti-līna* is the unmanifest cause of everything. That which transcends the *avyakta,* the unmanifest, *avyaktāt paraḥ,* that which is the *satya* of the *avyakta.*

Saḥ maheśvaraḥ. He is the limitless *parabrahman. Paraḥ saḥ* is sometimes mistakenly chanted as *parasya. Yaḥ parassa maheśvaraḥ.* Maheśvara is *parabrahman,* the *para-ātman.* That is the real *svarūpa.*

Kirtans

Vandehaṁ śāradām[20]

वन्देहं शारदाम्। विशारदां
ज्ञानदां वरदाम्। (वन्देहं शारदाम्) ॥
शुद्धसत्त्व-स्वरूपिणीम्।
स्वच्छहृदयनिवासिनीम्।
स्वप्रकाशरूपिणीम्। (वन्देहं शारदाम्) ॥
परापरविद्याभूषिताम्। सुरवरसुजनसेविताम्।
शुभदां सुलभाम्। सुस्वरवाद्यनिरताम्।
(वन्देहं शारदाम्) ॥

vandehaṁ śāradām, viśāradāṁ varadām,
jñānadāṁ (vandehaṁ śāradām).
śuddhasattva-svarūpiṇīm,
svacchahṛdayanivāsinīm,
svaprakāśarūpiṇīm, (vandehaṁ śāradām).
parāparavidyābhūṣitām,
suravarasujanasevitām,
śubhadāṁ sulabhām, susvaravādyaniratām,
(vandehaṁ śāradām).

I salute Goddess Śāradā, who is an expert in everything, who gives knowledge and boons, who is pure by nature, who abides in a pure mind, who is self-effulgent. I worship Goddess

[20] Composed by the author

Śāradā who is adorned with absolute and relative knowledge, who is sought by the ranked ones among the *deva*s and dispassionate seekers, who is easy to gain, who gives all that is auspicious, who gives knowledge to those who are free of likes and dislikes, who always remains in well-tuned instruments (of music), I worship Goddess Śāradā.

Vandehaṁ śāradām, ahaṁ śāradāṁ vande, with reverence I salute Goddess Śāradā. Another name for Goddess Sarasvatī is Śāradā, the one who bestows knowledge, *jñānaṁ dadāti.*

Viśāradām. If we bring in the prefix *vi*, that Śāradā becomes an expert in everything, *viśāradā. Jñānadā* is *jñānaṁ dadāti*, the one who confers knowledge. *Varadā* is *varaṁ dadāti*, the one who gives you protection, or the one who gives you boons.

Śuddhasattva-svarūpiṇīm. Śuddha is that which has no *mālinya*, uncleanliness, where there is no problem. *Sattva* which accounts for knowledge is conveyed by white colour. She is *śuddhasattva*, represented by white *mālā*, garland, white sari, white lotus seat, and white swan. She is all-knowledge. Knowledge is possible only when the mind is clear. That is why everything about her is white.

Svaccha-hṛdaya-nivāsinīm, she is the one who abides in a mind that is clean and pure. The mind is clean when one is not in the grip of *rāga-dveṣa*s, likes and dislikes. That kind of mind is called *svaccha-hṛdaya,* which can drop all its ideas and remain free to see, to learn. This is how we understand something new or see through a topic, reversing what was thought known. If the mind can abide in that kind of condition because of its freedom from the hold of likes and dislikes, we say it is a clean mind.

She is *svaprakāśa-rūpiṇī,* one who is self-effulgent, in the form of the *svaprakāśa-ātman,* which is the self.

Parāparavidyābhūṣitām. We have to learn two kinds of knowledge, *vidyā.* One is *apara-vidyā,* the various disciplines of knowledge in the sphere of things that we can objectify; and the other is *para-vidyā,* knowledge of the self. These two cover all knowledge. There is no third discipline of knowledge. That she is all-knowledge means she is both *para-vidyā* and *apara-vidyā.*

We worship her in a particular form. To do so is a privilege. In order to make the worship very real, it is good to have a form. It is not that the form is God, but rather, it is to God that we assign a given form. We worship the Lord, and not the form. It is a privilege that we can create an altar, that we can do a *pūjā.* We enjoy this privilege when we are born into a culture that worships the Lord in a form. We have to create that privilege or receive that privilege.

When Goddess Śāradā is worshipped, she adorns ornaments like bangles and earrings. However, her real adornments are *para* and *apara-vidyā. Parāparavidyābhūṣitām*, the one who is decked with the adornment, *bhūṣaṇa*, of the two *vidyā*s. She is not under the spell of this knowledge; it is something she wields. If you come under the spell of the knowledge, you become proud. If you wield the knowledge, you bear it lightly. This is true of any adornment like make-up, for example. If a person tries to cover up the face with make-up, it does not enhance the appearance so well, because the person considers it a problem when the make-up wears off. On the other hand, if a self-confident person puts on make-up, she does not have any problem with the make-up wearing off, because she accepts herself. She has nothing to cover up. It sits well with her. Even if one spends lot of time at the dressing table, one can be free when there is a degree of self-worth. If one does not accept oneself, any make-up is a load; it causes anxiety.

Suravara-sujana-sevitām. Even the *sura-vara*s, the greatest of the *devatā*s such as Indra in the *Kenopaniṣad*, seek that knowledge. Without that knowledge, they are simply *devatā*s comparing themselves with other *devatā*s.

Not all people may seek knowledge deliberately. They may want to know, but may not have a great value for knowledge. So they barter knowledge for the sake of wealth. Goddess Lakṣmī seems to be more important than knowledge for some. Others, however, may feel just the reverse. Such people are thinking people, *sujanas*, those who will give up Lakṣmī for knowledge.

Sulabhām means easy to gain. Goddess Sarasvatī is the easiest to gain because knowledge is already there. Lakṣmī is the result of effort, a *karmaphala*, something that has to be produced, *utpādya*. Even if you win a million dollars in a lottery, it is a *karmaphala*. You may think you did not do anything, but you had done enough earlier, which is why you got it and nobody else did. You always get what you work for; Lakṣmī is always a result of your effort, *karmaphala*. For knowledge, only the means of knoweldge needs to be available. If the means of knowledge is available, knowledge takes place. Understanding that 1+1=2 does not require either money or *karma*. It is a fact, but you will not know it until you are ready for it. So knowledge is always *sulabha*, easy to gain. All that is required is preparedness of mind.

Śubhadām. Śubha is that which lends finesse to your undertaking, like a grand finale. Anything that ends well is *śubha*, auspicious; and the real *śubha*, is *mokṣa*, the release from *saṁsāra*. Until then, the journey is on; the fight is on, the struggle is on.

When the *pramāṇa* and the mind are attuned properly, the meaning becomes clear. Even the *śāstra* becomes evident. Look before and look later, and the meaning clicks. If there is another meaning, that also clicks; that is *jñāna*. When things are in tune, things fall into place. You can get the melody you want from a musical instrument only when it is tuned well. All the notes are in harmony. Otherwise, each is a discordant note. In a well-tuned instrument, you see the Goddess, whether the instrument is musical or the human body-mind-sense-complex. She is *susvaravādyaniratām*. *Susvara* means an instrument that has its notes in concord. A *svara* is a note. A human body is considered to be a *vādya*, an instrument, like the flute. An Indian flute is a reed that belongs to the bamboo family. First, you cut the reed, and hollow it out, removing all the pith inside. Then you clean it and let it dry out completely before making the measured holes. It must produce that metallic sound. Then, when you blow into it, you have music! The whole body-mind complex is like that. When it is well tuned, there is no *rāga-dveṣa*, nothing clogging it. In such a person or a well-tuned, harmonious instrument, *susvaravādya*, she abides, *niratā*. I salute that Goddess Śāradā.

Dakṣiṇāmūrte amūrte[21]

दक्षिणामूर्ते अमूर्ते ।
सनकादिमुनिजन-हृन्मूर्ते । (दक्षिणामूर्ते अमूर्ते) ॥
आगमसार-परिपूर्ण-आत्म-जिज्ञासु-
मनोगत-मूर्ते । (दक्षिणामूर्ते अमूर्ते)
प्रसीद हृदीश अधीहि ब्रह्म ।
त्यक्तसर्वं युक्तात्मानम् ।
त्वच्चरणागतं माम् । (दक्षिणामूर्ते अमूर्ते)

dakṣiṇāmūrte amūrte,
sanakādimunijana-hṛnmūrte,
(dakṣiṇāmūrte amūrte).
āgamasāra-paripūrṇa- ātma-
jijñāsu-manogata-mūrte, (dakṣiṇāmūrte amūrte).
prasīda hṛdīśa adhīhi brahma,
tyaktasarvaṁ yuktātmānam,
tvaccaraṇāgataṁ mām,
(dakṣiṇāmūrte amūrte).

Oh Lord Dakṣiṇāmūrti. One who has no form (essentially), the one who filled the hearts of sages like Sanaka, Oh Lord Dakṣiṇāmūrti. Oh Lord, the one who abides in the mind of the seeker of knowledge of the limitless *ātman* which is the essence of

---

[21] Composed by the author

all the Vedas, Oh Lord Dakṣiṇāmūrti. Please bless me, teach me about Brahman, (I am) the one who has given up every other pursuit, the one who is steady and pure in mind, the one who has come to your feet, Oh Lord Dakṣiṇāmūrti.

As the story goes, there are four sages, the *sanakādi munis*, (Sanaka, Sanandana, Sanatsujāta and Sanatkumāra) who are the four original receipients of the *vidyā* from Lord Dakṣiṇāmūrti. They are *jīva*s and therefore they are very old. Every *jīva* is old. Just as we re-paint and fix up old houses, we keep on repairing the body until there comes a time when we cannot do that any more. Then the *jīva* condemns this body and builds another one. The *jīva* is very old, so old that he has no age. Only the body is born anew. The *jīva,* who is a tenant, keeps on changing his dwelling. He moves from place to place. All the *jīva*s are *anādi;* they have no beginning. They have the grace of the Lord, who is sitting under the *prapañca* tree.

The world is like a tree

The world is understandably likened to a tree. It is a good illustration. You see a tree and you see that it comes from an unmanifest condition. The banyan tree, for example, is a long-lasting tree whose branches are horizontal. It puts down adventitious roots and goes on extending its area and its life.

In the botanical gardens at Kolkatta, India, there is a huge banyan tree covering many acres. The original trunk of the tree is gone. In its place there is a pole with a signboard that says, "here was the original trunk!" It is amazing that it comes from a seed, which is so small! This tiny seed contains the entire tree. A mango seed is big, and so is an avocado seed, compared to the seed of the banyan tree. In the *Chāndogya Upaniṣad*, Śvetaketu is asked to open the *nyagrodha-phala*, the fruit of the banyan tree.

The teacher asks, "What do you see?"

"Rows and rows of seeds."

"Take out one seed."

Śvetaketu must have picked it up with a thorn. "Open it. What do you see?"

"Nothing."

"You are sitting under a banyan tree. Where did it come from?"

"It came from this kind of seed."

"But there is nothing in it."

"Everything is there in it."

It is programmed. In its causal form, in the form of a seed, the whole tree is unmanifest. Given the time and place that is necessary, it becomes manifest, *vyakta*. Manifestation, *abhivyakti*, does not take place unless the conditions are conducive. So too is knowledge.

One cannot thrust knowledge into someone. One does not create knowledge, constructing it on the slabs of ignorance. Instead, under the right conditions, the ignorance goes away, like even clouds rolling away to reveal the sun. Under the right conditions that one creates, ignorance goes away. One needs to create those conditions. That is where will is necessary.

From unmanifest to manifest, *avyakta* to *vyakta*, is a cycle such as from the tree to the seed to the tree. This is how *sṛṣṭi* of *jagat* is. From the cause, it is manifest with all the details. The banyan tree is the *jagat*, the world and the Lord together. Here, the *jagat* is pointed out as a tree, *vṛkṣa*. It has this manifest form with foliage and branches.

You see the tree standing. You do not see its roots. There is a taproot that goes deep into the ground. Do you need to see the roots to accept that the tree has them? No. Is it a belief? No. A belief is subject to correction on verification. This is *abādhitaṁ jñānam*, knowledge that cannot be negated. Similarly, you do not just believe that there is God. You know that there is God. You do not know what kind of root system there is beneath the surface, but you know that it is there, *asti*. How is it, *katham asti*? In what form is it, *kiṁ rūpeṇa asti*? What is its nature, *svarūpa*? That is what you have to know.

Ūrdhva-mūlam (*Bhagavad Gītā* 15-1), the root of the tree of universe is above. The root is not above, but beyond your mind, beyond your senses. Still you know that it is there. That is what the cause is. The effect is the tree. Under this tree, *vṛkṣa,* all the *jīva*s symbolised by the *sanakādi muni*s are seated, seeking knowledge from the Lord who is the source of all-knowledge.

The Lord as the guru

The Lord himself is the *guru*. Then why don't we go directly to the Lord? Suppose you perform penance and get to see God and ask him for self-knowledge. He will ask you to go to a teacher. He cannot improve upon his own words that you are the whole. That is the only knowledge. Everything else is just a working conclusion. Knowledge of anything is knowledge of only a facet of it; you don't see it through all the way. An entire scientific career is spent on knowing one small facet of knowledge in science. The whole does not have any parts. If it has parts, your knowledge is partial! This partless whole happens to be you. It cannot be separate from you. This is the only knowledge that does not leave anything to be desired.

We are talking of a tradition in which the Lord is presented as a teacher. He is sitting under the *prapañca* tree and the *sanakādi* students are seated around him. He is addressed as *dakṣiṇāmūrte amūrte,* the one who is free from all forms, and yet, is all forms.

Sanakādimunijana-hṛnmūrte. In the original composition, it was *hṛtpūrte.* It means one who fills the hearts of *sanakādi-munijana,* the sages beginning with Sanaka. He is the one who made the *jīva*s discover their own *pūrṇatva,* completeness. These two compounds are in the vocative case, addressing Lord Dakṣiṇāmūrti. If we take it as being *hṛnmūrte,* it can mean the one whose form is in the hearts of the sages beginning with Sanaka.

Further, he is addressed as *jijñāsu-manogata-mūrte,* the one who obtains in the heart of a *jijñāsu.* A *jijñāsu* is the one who constantly invokes the grace of Śrī Dakṣiṇāmūrti in order to know. What does he want to know? He is *ātma-jijñāsu,* one who wants to know the self, *ātman.* What kind of *ātman*? The limitless self, *paripūrṇa-ātman,* which is the subject matter of Vedanta, the *āgamasāra.*

Prasīda, please bless me. *Hṛdīśa,* Oh! The Lord of my heart. I recognise him as the one who obtains in my heart.

Adhīhi brahma, please teach me about Brahman. This word, *adhīhi,* suggests the *vākya,* sentence, in *Taittirīyopaniṣad.*

भृगुर्वै वारुणिः। वरुणं पितरमुपससार। अधीहि भगवो ब्रह्मेति॥

bhṛgurvai vāruṇiḥ, varuṇaṁ pitaram upasasāra, adhīhi bhagavo brahmeti.

Bhṛgu, the well-known son of Varuṇa, approached his father Varuṇa with the request, "O revered sir, teach me Brahman" [22]

Tyaktasarva is the one who gives up everything. This knowledge is at the top of the list of priorities; everything else has gone down. This is well-ascertained understanding, the *vyavasāyātmikā buddhiḥ* (*Bhagavad Gītā* 2-41, 44). For whom is it so?

Yuktātmānam. For the one who is clear-headed, and in possession of his faculties–*yuktaḥ ātmā antaḥkaraṇaṁ yasya,* the one whose mind is fit.

Tvaccaraṇāgataṁ mām, to me, the one who has come to your feet. I have sought your feet, *tvat caraṇau āgataṁ mām.* Please teach me.

We ask Śrī Dakṣiṇāmūrti to bless us with this knowledge. It is he who provides the teacher. We need his grace for the teaching to become real.

---

[22] (*Taittirīya Upaniṣad* 3-1-1)

Khelati mama hṛdaye

Swami Sadāśiva Brahmendra's famous composition goes as follows:

खेलति मम हृदये रामः खेलति मम हृदये
मोह-महार्णव-तारक-कारी
राग-द्वेष-मुखासुर-मारि ।
शान्ति-विदेह-सुता-सहचारी
दहरायोध्या-नगर-विहारी (खेलति मम ...)
परमहंस-साम्राज्योद्धारी
सत्य-ज्ञानानन्द-शरीरी ॥ (खेलति मम ...)

khelati mama hṛdaye rāmaḥ khelati mama hṛdaye
moha-mahārṇava-tāraka-kārī
rāga-dveṣa-mukhāsura-māri,
śānti-videha-sutā-sahacārī
daharāyodhyā-nagara-vihārī, (khelati mama ...)
paramahaṁsa-sāmrājyoddhārī
satya-jñānānanda-śarīrī. (khelati mama ...)

Rāma dances in my heart. He is wedded to *śānti*, born of freedom gained from the knowledge that the self is not the body and the one who shines in the invincible city of the space in my heart, who dances in my heart. Rāma crossed the great ocean of delusion and destroyed the demons of likes and dislikes. He, whose nature is of *satyam, jñānam* and *anantam*, re-establishes the kingdom of *sādhus* (helps you attain *śānti*).

In the story of the *Rāmāyaṇa*, Lord Rāma married Sītādevī and went to the forest where Rāvaṇa kidnapped Sītādevī. To get her back, Lord Rāma had to wage a war. He destroyed Rāvaṇa and Kumbhakarṇa, his brother, and then returned to his kingdom and established himself on the throne. His rule is called *rāmarājya*. This is the story of *Rāmāyaṇa*. We can understand it symbolically in terms of the self.

Ramante yasmin iti rāmaḥ, the one in whom you discover joy is Rāma. He is the *saccidānanda-svarūpaḥ*. He is wedded to Sītādevī, who is *śānti*, peace. She is Vaidehī, the daughter of *videha*, the one who is free from the identification with the body. *Śānti* obtains in a person whose self is not mistaken for the body. This *śānti* is Vaidehi. She is the *ātma-śānti* that is the *svarūpa* of the *ātman*.

Rāvaṇa and Kumbhakarṇa are the binding likes and dislikes, *rāga-dveṣa*s. They kidnapped *śānti* and kept her away from Rāma, the *ātman*. Where? In an island, in the ocean of *moha*, delusion. With the help of Lord Rāma you destroy the Rāvaṇa, Kumbhakarṇa, *rāga-dveṣa*s, and get back Sītā, *śānti*. You can then establish a *sāṁrājya*, complete sovereignty of the self from the capital of Ayodhyā, a city that cannot be seized by anybody, *yoddhuṁ aśakyā ayodhyā*.

Where is this invincible city? *Dahara,* in the space within, in my *buddhi.*

Paramahaṁsa-sāṁrājyoddhāri, he re-established the *sāṁrājya,* the kingdom of *sādhus.* Lord Rāma is *ājānu-bahu, kodaṇḍa-pāṇi, dyutimān,* etc. What is the body, *śarira,* of this Rāma? He is *satya-jñāna-ānanda-śarīrī*: His *śarīra* is *satyaṁ-jñānam-anantam,* the reality of every body in the form of limitless consciousness.

Religious Festivals

Sarasvatī pūjā

When you worship Īśvara, you are Brahman as an individual, and the altar is the same Brahman with *māyā-śakti* manifesting as the *sarvajña*, all-knowledge. Even though the essential truth of both is *satyaṁ jñānam anataṁ brahma*, you are invoking the Lord who is *sarvajña*, all-knowledge, *sarvaśakti*, all-power. Invoking this Lord, who is all-knowledge, as a remover of obstacles, Gaṇeśa, as Goddess of knowledge, Sarasvatī, as bestower of all *puruṣārtha*s, Parameśvara in both Śiva and Viṣṇu, is common to all Hindus. There are special days in Hindu calendar for offering special worship to different deities. On the ninth day of the Dasara, a 10-day festival of Śakti, the Lord is invoked as all-knowledge Sarasvatī. A special altar is created with books and instruments of music like *vīṇā*, flute, drums and so on.

The tenth day is Vijayadaśamī, when all the work tools are worshipped. It is called *āyudha-pūjā*. On this Vijayadaśamī day, even the most dusty smithy place is made worthy of *pūjā*, with all the hammers, tongs, anvil and bellows neatly arranged to make an altar. *Candana*, *kuṅkuma*, turmeric, and flowers make the whole place a temple. On that day, all the buses are adorned with lots of flowers, sandal paste and vermilion. In all cities, the drivers do the *pūjā* in the morning before they start work. Even in government undertakings, any machine such as a word-processor is worshipped. There is knowledge of skill involved in every tool, even in a simple spanner. While we worship knowledge, books and musical instruments on the *Sarasvatī-pūjā* day, we also worship all the tools that help us in getting things done.

Everything is sacred

It takes certain way of looking at things, to worship books and tools. The vision of Īśvara being what it is, this is all possible and meaningful. His manifold *śakti* is worshipped, acknowledging as well as invoking the grace.

The books that make the altar for worship need not be Vedas and *Purāṇas*; they can be of any discipline of knowledge. When the children keep their books at the altar and participate in the *pūjā*, their attitude towards knowledge is going to be different. The concept of sacred becomes all inclusive. This is possible only when you get your vision of Īśvara straight. You cannot worship a tool if you dub it as dumb. There is knowledge, an order involved. If the spanner is not an appropriate tool because of its size, it cannot get the job of tightening a nut done. There is law and order involved and all of this is Bhagavān.

From childhood, you learn to appreciate and look upon things as sacred. This is so for all Hindus. They may not know Vedanta, but they certainly do know that everything is sacred. Everyone will say "*sab bhagavān hai,* everything is Bhagavān." They may not have all the answers, but their attitude reflects the imbibed sense.

Navarātri festival in Tamil Nadu

In Tamil Nadu, many homes organise a *golu* during the *navarātri* festival. They assemble nine steps and on those steps, they display various forms made of clay, wood, etc. You will find the whole world there. You will even find a doll of an Englishman on those steps. The top step is for *devatā*s such as Brahmā, Viṣṇu and Śiva. On the next step you will see Gaṇeśa and so on. Then you will have the *yakṣa*s, *kinnara*s, angels, as they are described in the books. Then you will find all types of human beings; people from different countries and cultures, wearing different kinds of costumes. You will then find different kinds of animals, trees, and fruits. The whole *jagat* is there. It is the *jagad-rūpiṇī-śakti.* In some houses, they will bring in modern technology such as a train track with trains running, water fountains, and so on.

Women call each other to visit their home and say, "Please visit my home and make it sacred." The well-dressed visiting women are asked to sing at this altar of *golu*. Every song is, of course, in praise of the Lord. This is the popular festival of nine nights, *navarātri*.

In every culture, there are a few festivals with certain forms of expression. If these expressions and customs are removed, life will be robotic. These things demonstrate and re-establish certain values and attitudes, enriching one's life.

Rāmanavamī

Let us look at some verses about Lord Rāma from the *Vālmīki Rāmāyaṇa*.

कूजन्तं राम रामेति मधुरं मधुराक्षरम्।
आरुह्य कविताशाखां वन्दे वाल्मीकिकोकिलम्॥

kūjantaṁ rāma rāmeti madhuraṁ madhurākṣaram,
āruhya kavitāśākhāṁ vande vālmīkikokilam.

I salute Vālmīki, who is likened to a cuckoo that is perched upon the branch of poetry, singing the sweetest word, Rāma, again and again.

Vande (I salute) the *kokila*, cuckoo bird, the bird that has sweet warbles. Vālmīki is a bard, the *kokila*, *kūjantam*, singing, *rāma rāma iti*. The word Rāma is considered to be a very sweet word. It is the *madhuraṁ madhurākṣaram*, that which is the sweetest word. *Āruhya kavitāśākhām*, the bird, Vālmīki, is perched, *āruhya*, upon the branch of poetry, *kavitā-śākhā*. (*Vālmīki Rāmāyaṇa Dhyana śloka*)

The *Rāmāyaṇa* was always sung. The *Uttara Rāmāyaṇa* is something different. it is said that *Rāmāyaṇa* was first sung by Lava and Kuśa in the court of Lord Rāma, without knowing that Rāma was their father. The claim is that Vālmīki taught these children. The *Rāmāyaṇa* ends with Śrī Rāma's coronation, *paṭṭābhiṣeka*, and everything else seems to be an addition.

In fact, the *Rāmāyaṇa* starts with a dialogue between Vālmīki and Nārada. Vālmīki was a poet, but originally, he was a dacoit who used to rob people to support his wife and parents. One day Sage Nārada happened to come that way and was stopped by Vālmīki. Nārada parted with whatever he had and asked Vālmīki why he was a robber. When Vālmīki replied that he made his living that way, Nārada pointed out that there must be another way to make a living. Vālmīki said that this was the only way he knew.

"But this is *pāpa*," Nārada said.

"What is *pāpa*?" Vālmīki asked.

"It is the result of wrong action."

"How can you say that this is wrong?"

"Would you want to be robbed?"

"No."

"Then it is wrong."

"Oh. What will happen then?"

"It will give you unpleasant situations in this life and in future lives."

Vālmīki was frightened, but thought, "After all, there are three others in the household who will share my *pāpa*."

"No," Nārada told him. "You alone reap all the *pāpa*. Go and ask them."

Vālmīki went and asked his father if he would share his *pāpa*.

"No," his father said. "I have my own load to carry and I do not want to carry yours."

The mother said, "No. It is your duty to take care of us. We are old, and we are not going to take your *pāpa*."

Vālmīki then thought that may be his wife would share his *pāpa*. She also refused. "You are supposed to bring things, and I am supposed to take care of the house. How can you earn your money doing a wrong thing? I am not going to receive any share from your *pāpa*."

Vālmīki became wiser and asked Nārada what he should do to get rid of his *pāpa*. Nārada asked him to repeat the name of Śrī Rāma. Vālmīki repeated the *rāma-nāma* and only the *rāma-nāma*. It is a beautiful word for chanting. Vālmīki went on to become a saint.

The story goes that he became so still that the ants built an anthill around him. Nārada came back to that place years later and heard the *rāma-śabda* coming out of a *valmīka*, anthill. He arrived at the source, cleared it and found Vālmīki. This was sage Vālmīki. Again, Nārada is the one who first tells him the entire story of Rāma in brief. That becomes the basis of Vālmīki's expansion of the story into poetry. Let us look at the first verse.

> तपःस्वाध्यायनिरतं तपस्वी वाग्विदां वरम् ।
> नारदं परिपप्रच्छ वाल्मीकिर्मुनिपुङ्गवम् ॥
>
> *tapaḥsvādhyāyaniratam̐ tapasvī vāgvidām̐ varam,*
> *nāradam̐ paripapraccha vālmīkir muni-puṅgavam.*
>
> Vālmīki, the ascetic, being engaged in religious austerities, asked Nārada, who revels in study and contemplation, the most exalted of the sages, the one who is best among the eloquent (1-1-1).

Vālmīkiḥ tapasvī nāradam̐ munipuṅgavam̐ paripapraccha. Paripapraccha, Vālmīki asked him properly. Whom did he ask? *Nāradam*, he asked Nārada, the *munipuṅgava*, the one who is the most exalted of the sages, and *vāgvidāṁ vara*, the one who is unexcelled among the eloquent speakers, one who is always committed to religious discipline, *tapas*, *svādhyāya*, study of the *śāstra*, etc. Who is the *tapasvin*? It is Vālmīki, who sat under a tree and chanted Lord Rāma's name. What did he ask of Nārada?

को न्वस्मिन् सांप्रतं लोके गुणवान् कश्च वीर्यवान्।
धर्मज्ञश्च कृतज्ञश्च सत्यवाक्यो दृढव्रतः॥

ko nvasmin sāmprataṁ loke guṇavān
kaśca vīryavān,
dharmajñaśca kṛtajñaśca satyavākyo
dṛḍhavrataḥ.

Nowadays, in this world, who is that person who has all the virtues and who is also a person of valour, who knows what *dharma* is and who is most grateful, truthful and of firm resolve? (1-1-2).

Asmin loke, in this world, *sāmpratam*, nowadays, *kaḥ*, who is that person, who is *guṇavān*, the one who has all the virtues, *kaḥ ca vīryavān*, who is also a person of valour. He wants to hear of that kind of person. Nārada knows it all. He is a *triloka-sancāri*, one who can travel across all the three worlds.

Dharmajñaḥ ca kṛtajñaḥ ca satya vākyo dṛḍhavrataḥ. Who is the *dharmajña*, the one who knows what *dharma* is and what *adharma* is very clearly, who is a *kṛtajña*, one who never forgets whatever is *kṛtam*, done to him; in other words, who is grateful. Who is the *satya-vākya*, the one whose statements, *vākya*, are always true, *satya*. Whatever he says also becomes true. There are two types of *satya-vākya*. One is saying what one knows to be true. The other is, whatever one says comes true. A *dṛḍhavrata* is one whose resolves are always firm.

> चारित्रेण च को युक्तः सर्वभूतेषु को हितः ।
> विद्वान् कः कः समर्थश्च कश्चैकप्रियदर्शनः ॥
>
> *cāritreṇa ca ko yuktaḥ sarvabhūteṣu ko hitaḥ,*
> *vidvān kaḥ kaḥ samarthaś ca*
> *kaścaikapriyadarśanaḥ.*
>
> Who lives an illustrious life, who is committed to the welfare of all living beings? Who is the one who is a scholar and a wise person? Who is powerful and at the same time very pleasing to see? (1-1-3).

Cāritreṇa ca ko yuktaḥ sarva bhūteṣu ko hitaḥ, who lives an illustrious life characterised by compassion and doing good to all beings. *Vidvān kaḥ*, who is the one who is a *paṇḍita*, a scholar and a wise person? *Kaḥ samarthaḥ ca*, who is the one who is capable? *Kaḥ ca eka-priyadarśanaḥ*, who is the one who is also very pleasing to see, pleasing to the eye?

आत्मवान् को जितक्रोधो द्युतिमान् कोऽनसूयकः।
कस्य बिभ्यति देवाश्च जातरोषस्य संयुगे॥

ātmavān ko jitakrodho dyutimān ko'nasūyakaḥ,
kasya bibhyati devāśca jātaroṣasya saṁyuge.

Who has mastery over his body and sense organs and has mastered his anger? Who is well-known and not fault-finding? Who do the very Gods dread when his wrath is provoked in the battle? (1-1-4).

Ātmavān kaḥ. All this describes one person. *Ātmavān* does not mean *saccidānanda-ātmavān*. Everyone is an *ātmavān* by that definition. *Ātmavān* is he who has the *ātmā*, the body and senses, *dehendriyasaṅghāta*, in his hands, the person who has control over his *deha*, body and his *indriyas*, sense organs. *Jitakrodaḥ* is he who has mastered his anger. *Dyutimān* is one who looks brilliant. *Anasūyakaḥ*, one who does not look for some *doṣa*, blemish, where there is virtue, *guṇa*. *Guṇeṣu doṣadarśanam* is finding a fault where there are *guṇas*, good qualities. That is called *asūya*. An *asūyakaḥ* is like a proofreader. *Anasūyakaḥ* is one who does not have *asūyā*.

Kasya bibhyati devāḥ, jātaroṣasya, of whom, when roused to indignation, *saṁyuge*, in battle, even the *devas* are afraid. He who is such a man of *dharma* that if he has the *roṣa*, the indignation, that something has to be done in order to protect *dharma*, in the battlefield, *saṁyuge*, even the *deva*s run away. Such a person was Lord Rāma.

एतदिच्छाम्यहं श्रोतुं परं कौतूहलं हि मे।
महर्षे त्वं समर्थोऽसि ज्ञातुमेवंविधं नरम्॥

etat icchāmyaham śrotuṁ paraṁ
kautūhalaṁ hi me,
maharṣe tvaṁ samartho'si jñātum-
evaṁvidhaṁ naram.

I wish to hear this, Oh great sage! You are in a position to know such a man and I am very enthusiastic to know about him (1-1-5).

Etadicchāmi ahaṁ śrotum, I want to hear this, *maharṣe,* Oh great sage, *tvaṁ samartho'si*, you are in a position to know this. I am very enthusiastic to know this, *kautūhalaṁ me*. I want you to talk about someone who is like this now, *sāmpratam*, as opposed to in the past. I know that you must know a person who is like this, *jñātum evaṁ vidhaṁ naram*; because you have been traveling a lot. Therefore, you should have met somebody in one of the three *loka*s. *Kaḥ*, who is that person? Thus did Vālmīki ask Nārada.

Nārada wanted a *kāvya* out of Vālmīki. Therefore, he gave him an account of Lord Rāma's story.

श्रुत्वा चैतत्त्रिलोकज्ञो वाल्मीकेर्नारदो वचः।
श्रूयतामिति चामन्त्र्य प्रहृष्टो वाक्यमब्रवीत्॥

śrutvā caitat-trilokajño vālmīker-nārado vacaḥ,
śrūyatāmiti cāmantrya prahṛṣṭo vākyam abravīt.

Having heard these words of Vālmīki, Nārada, the one who knows what is happening in all the three worlds, being happy, having addressed him, "Please listen," spoke the following words (1-1-6).

Śrutvā ca etat vacaḥ, having heard these words, *vālmīkeḥ*, of Vālmīki, Nārada, the one who knows what is happening in all the three worlds, *trilokajñaḥ*, addressing him, *āmantrya*, "Please listen," *prahṛṣṭaḥ*, being so happy, *vākyam abravīt*, spoke these words.

बहवो दुर्लभाश्चैव ये त्वया कीर्तिता गुणाः।
मुने वक्ष्याम्यहं बुद्ध्वा तैर्युक्तः श्रूयतां नरः॥

bahavo durlabhāś caiva ye tvayā kīrtitā guṇāḥ,
mune vakṣyāmyahaṁ buddhvā tairyuktaḥ śrūyatāṁ naraḥ.

Oh sage! I shall tell you of such a person, who is endowed with the manifold and rare good qualities that have been described by you (1-1-7).

He mune, Oh Vālmīki! A *muni* is someone who is capable of proper thinking, *manana-śīlaḥ*. *Bahavaḥ*, there are too many. *Guṇāḥ*, good qualities. *Durlabhāḥ*, they are not easily found (in one). These good qualities, which are difficult to acquire, which have been praised by you, *ye tvayā kīrtitāḥ*, I will tell, *vakṣyāmi aham*, of a man who is described, *taiḥ uktaḥ naraḥ*, who is endowed with those *guṇa*s, knowing, *buddhvā*, that person. There is a person who has all these qualities and a few more. *Śrūyatām*, listen.

इक्ष्वाकुवंशप्रभवो रामो नाम जनैः श्रुतः ।
नियतात्मा महावीर्यो द्युतिमान् धृतिमान् वशी ॥

ikṣvākuvaṁśaprabhavo rāmo
nāma janaiḥ śrutaḥ,
niyatātmā mahāvīryo dyutimān
dhṛtimān vaśī.

There is one born into the family of Ikṣvāku, very well-known by the people, and who is known by the name of Rāma. He has his body, mind and sense organs under his control, is very powerful, radiant, a man of fortitude (1-1-8).

Ikṣvāku-vaṁśa-prabhavaḥ, the one who is born into the family of Ikṣvāku. *Rāmo nāma janaiḥ śrutaḥ*, the one who is very well-known and called by his people as Rāma. *Niyata-ātmā*, one whose body and sense organs are under his control. He is *mahāvīryaḥ*, person of extraordinary strength. *Dyutimān*, a radiant person, *dhṛtimān*, a man of fortitude, courage.

Vaśī, he keeps his mind also under control, not just his body and senses.

बुद्धिमान् नीतिमान् वाग्मी श्रीमाञ्छत्रुनिबर्हणः ।
विपुलांसो महाबाहुः कंबुग्रीवो महाहनुः ॥

buddhimān nītimān vāgmī śrīmāñchatru-nibarhaṇaḥ,
vipulāṁso mahābāhuḥ kaṁbugrīvo mahāhanuḥ.

He is intelligent, who has justice, who is eloquent, resourceful, and can eliminate his enemies easily. He is distinguished, with broad shoulders, powerful arms, appropriate neck and strong jaws (1-1-9).

Buddhimān, he is one who has *buddhi*. Everyone has *buddhi*, but then it has to be properly used. Here is a person who uses his *buddhi* properly. *Nītimān*, one who knows and follows justice. *Vāgmī*, one who can communicate. *Śrīmān*, one who has *śrī*, wealth. *Śatru-nibarhaṇaḥ*, one who can eliminate all the enemies. *Vipulāṁsaḥ*, broad-shouldered. *Mahābāhuḥ*, one who has long hands. *Kambu-grīvaḥ*, *kambu* is conch-like, *grīvā*, neck. It means one whose neck is neither too big nor too small. *Mahāhanuḥ*, the one who has a strong jaw, does not look weak.

महोरस्को महेष्वासो गूढजत्रुररिन्दमः ।
आजानुबाहुः सुशिराः सुललाटः सुविक्रमः ॥

mahorasko maheṣvāso gūḍhajatrur arindamaḥ,
ājānubāhuḥ suśirāḥ sulalāṭaḥ suvikramaḥ.

He is marked by his broad chest, mighty bow, and a well-covered collarbone, and is capable of keeping his enemies under control. His long arms extend right upto his knees. He has a well-formed head, a shapely forehead, and a charming gait (1-1-10).

Mahoraskaḥ, the one who has a broad-chest. *Maheṣvāsaḥ*, one whose bow is big. Just looking at the bow, people will run away. *Gūḍhajatruḥ*, one whose bones are well covered. *Arindamaḥ*, the one who keeps the enemies under control. *Ājānubāhuḥ,* his arms are long coming down to his knees. *Suśirāḥ*, one whose head is beautifully shaped. *Sulalāṭaḥ,* there is ample *lalāṭa*, forehead. *Suvikramaḥ,* one who has graceful strides.

समः समविभक्ताङ्गः स्निग्धवर्णः प्रतापवान् ।
पीनवक्षा विशालाक्षो लक्ष्मीवाञ्छुभलक्षणः ॥

samaḥ samavibhakta-aṅgaḥ snigdhavarṇaḥ pratāpavān,
pīnavakṣā viśālākṣo lakṣmīvāñchubhalakṣaṇaḥ.

He is of composure, has well proportioned limbs, has a nice complexion, is mighty, has a wide chest, large eyes, has all the wealth, and has all the auspicious marks on his body (1-1-11).

Samaḥ, one who is the same in all situations, does not lose himself. *Samavibhakta-aṅgaḥ*, all the limbs are proportionate. *Snigdha-varṇaḥ*, of pleasing colour. *Pratāpavān*, one who has great power, bravery, etc. *Pīnavakṣā* means one who has a wide chest and *viśālākṣaḥ*, whose eyes are beautiful. *Lakṣmīvān*, one who has all the wealth. *Śubha-lakṣaṇaḥ*, he has all the auspicious marks, *lakṣaṇa*s. There is a book called *Sāmudrikā Lakṣaṇam*, which describes all the *lakṣaṇa*s a human being should have. Lord Rāma has all the noble *lakṣaṇa*s described in that book.

धर्मज्ञः सत्यसंधश्च प्रजानां च हिते रतः ।
यशस्वी ज्ञानसम्पन्नः शुचिर्वश्यः समाधिमान् ॥

dharmajñaḥ satyasandhaśca prajānāṁ
ca hite rataḥ,
yaśasvī jñānasampannaḥ śucir vaśyaḥ
samādhimān

He knows *dharma*, is committed to truth, always delights in the good of all his subjects. He is well-known, knows the *śāstra*s, pure, a man of self-control and well-absorbed mind (1-1-12).

Dharmajñaḥ, the one who knows *dharma*. One may know *dharma*, but one may not follow it. Therefore, there is also the word *satya-sandhaḥ* to describe Lord Rāma as one who is committed to *satya*, truth.

The word, *satya* stands for all other values. *Prajānāṁ ca hite rataḥ,* the one who is always sensitive to the *hita,* the good of all the *prajās,* subjects. *Yaśasvī,* the one who is well respected by one and all. *Jñāna-sampannaḥ,* one who has *śāstra-jñāna. Śuciḥ,* the one who is clean inside and out. *Vaśyaḥ,* the one who has everything under his control. *Samādhimān,* the one whose mind is composed.

प्रजापतिसमः श्रीमान् धाता रिपुनिषूदनः।
रक्षिता जीवलोकस्य धर्मस्य परिरक्षिता॥

prajāpatisamaḥ śrīmān dhātā ripuniṣūdanaḥ,
rakṣitā jīvalokasya dharmasya parirakṣitā.

He is a supporter of creation like Brahmāji, who has all the riches, nourisher (of the world), chastiser of those who are committed to *adharma,* protector of all living beings, and a staunch defender of *dharma* (1-1-13).

Prajāpati-samaḥ, the one who is like Brahmāji. *Śrīmān dhātā,* one who has wealth and is a great nourisher. *Ripu-niṣūdanaḥ,* one who is like fire to those committed to *adharma. Rakṣitā jīvalokasya,* he is the one protector of all living beings, not just mankind. *Dharmasya parirakṣitā,* he is the protector of *dharma* even if it means giving up of his life.

रक्षिता स्वस्य धर्मस्य स्वजनस्य च रक्षिता।
वेदवेदाङ्गतत्त्वज्ञो धनुर्वेदे च निष्ठितः॥

> *rakṣitā svasya dharmasya sva janasya ca rakṣitā,*
> *vedavedāṅgatattvajño dhanurvede ca niṣṭhitaḥ.*
>
> He is the protector (follower) of his own *dharma* and the protector of his people too, in terms of their life of *dharma*. He knows the truth of the Vedas and the *Vedāṅga*s, and is master of archery (1-1-14).

Rakṣitā svasya dharmasya, the protector of his own *dharma;* in the process of protecting all the people, he does not give up his own *dharma, svadharma*. *Sva-janasya ca rakṣitā,* the protector of his own people. When you become a politician, you generally forget your children. Politicians become so inspired by the problems in the society that they forget their own children and their own family. The observance of *dharma* starts at home. *Sva-jana* means one's own family members. As a king he has to protect the people who follow *dharma* from the law-breakers.

Now he begins to describe the kind of intellect Lord Rāma has. *Veda-vedāṅga-tattvajñaḥ,* he is the one who knows the subject matter of both the Vedas and the works that are ancillary to the Vedas, the *vedāṅga*s. *Dhanurvede ca niṣṭhitaḥ,* the one who is well-established with reference to knowledge of archery and warfare, the *dhanurveda*, an *upa-veda*.

> सर्वशास्त्रार्थतत्त्वज्ञः स्मृतिमान् प्रतिभानवान्।
> सर्वलोकप्रियः साधुरदीनात्मा विचक्षणः॥

sarvaśāstrārtha-tattvajñaḥ smṛtimān pratibhānavān,
sarvaloka-priyaḥ sādhur adīnātmā vicakṣaṇaḥ.

He knows and remembers the real meaning of all the scriptures and lives according to the scriptures. He is loved by all people, helpful to others, does not feel helpless at any time, and very dexterous (1-1-15).

Sarva-śāstra-artha-tattvajñaḥ, the one who knows the meaning of all the *śāstra*s, all the different disciplines of knowledge. *Smṛtimān*, not only does he know, he also remembers. *Pratibhānavān*—this means the one who can not only grasp and remember the wisdom of the *śāstra*s, but also the wisdom is available at the time of its need. *Sarva-loka-priyaḥ, sarvasya lokasya priyaḥ*—beloved to all. *Sarvaḥ lokaḥ priyaḥ yasya*—the entire world is beloved for whom. *Sādhuḥ, para-kāryaṁ sādhnoti iti sādhuḥ*, the one who is helpful to others, is a *sādhu*. *Adīnātmā*, one who does not feel helpless at any time. *Dīnātmā* means helpless; *adīnātmā* does not have this sense of helplessness. *Vicakṣaṇaḥ* means prowess, *samarthaḥ*, one who is dexterous and highly skilled in different situations.

सर्वदाभिगतः सद्भिः समुद्र इव सिन्धुभिः ।
आर्यः सर्वसमश्चैव सदैव प्रियदर्शनः ॥

sarvadābhigataḥ sadbhiḥ samudra iva sindhubhiḥ,
āryaḥ sarvasamaḥ caiva sadaiva priyadarśanaḥ.

He is always sought by the good, as the ocean is by all rivers. He is worshipful, equipoised, and is always loving and compassionate (1-1-16).

Sarvadā abhigataḥ sadbhiḥ, the one who is always sought after by the good, by everyone, in fact. How? *Samudra iva sindhubhiḥ*. Just as all the rivers search for the ocean and reach it, so too, all the good people *satpuruṣa*s seek Lord Rāma. He also receives them as they come, just as the ocean, *samudra*, would, the rivers.

Āryaḥ means *pūjyaḥ*, worshipful. *Sarvasamaḥ ca eva*, one who is equal to all or who is impartial while responding to people and upholds justice. *Sadaiva priyadarśanaḥ*, the one who always looks at people lovingly, whose looks are imbued with love and compassion.

स च सर्वगुणोपेतः कौसल्यानन्दवर्धनः ।
समुद्र इव गाम्भीर्ये धैर्येण हिमवानिव ॥

sa ca sarvaguṇopetaḥ kausalyānandavardhanaḥ,
samudra iva gāmbhīrye dhairyeṇa himavān iva.

He is endowed with all the virtues, and enhances the delight of his mother, Kausalyā.

He vies with the ocean in dignity and is comparable to the himālayas in firmness (1-1-17).

Sarvaguṇopetaḥ, the one who has all the *guṇa*s, noble attributes like *amānitva*, absence of demand for respect, and so on.[23] *Kausalyā-ānanda-vardhanaḥ*, the one who makes Kausalyā's happiness grow every day. *Gāmbhīrya* is dignity. He has a dignity that comes out of a fullness that is like the fullness of the ocean, *samudra iva. Dhairyeṇa himavān iva*, in courage and firmness, he is like Himavān, the Himālayas.

विष्णुना सदृशो वीर्ये सोमवत्प्रियदर्शनः ।
कालाग्निसदृशः क्रोधे क्षमया पृथ्वीसमः ॥

viṣṇunā sadṛśo vīrye somavat-priya-darśanaḥ,
kālāgnisadṛśaḥ krodhe kṣamayā pṛthvī-samaḥ.

In strength, he is equal to Viṣṇu; he is very pleasing to see like the moon; in anger, he is like the fire that melts everything at the time of *pralaya;* in forebearance, he is equal to mother earth (1-1-18).

Viṣṇunā sadṛśo vīrye. In strength, *vīrya*, he is equal to Lord Viṣṇu. Does he look fierce and stern? No. *Somavat priya-darśanaḥ*, like the moon, he is very

[23] For a discussion of such values refer the author's book 'The Value of Values' based on the *Bhagavad Gītā*, Chapter 13.

pleasing to see. *Kālāgni sadṛśaḥ krodhe,* he has a righteous anger, because he is a king, and this anger is like *kālāgni,* the fire that melts everything at the time of *pralaya,* dissolution. *Kṣamayā pṛthivī samaḥ*. In *kṣamā,* he is equal to *pṛthivī,* earth. *Kṣamā* is patience, forbearance and the capacity to pardon. The mother earth is always praised for foreberance. How much sin is committed against and on the earth! Yet, the patient earth keeps on giving to us; the roses are still fragrant, the wheat continues to be nutritious.

> धनदेन समस्त्यागे सत्ये धर्म इवापरः ... ॥
>
> *dhanadena samaḥ tyāge satye dharma iva aparaḥ...*
>
> In giving he is equal to Kubera and in speaking the truth, he is like another deity of *dharma.* (1-1-19).

Dhanadena samaḥ tyāge, in giving, *tyāga,* he is like Kubera, the lord of the exchequer. Here, *tyāga* is charity, *dānam. Satye dharma iva aparaḥ,* in speaking the truth, *satya-bhāṣaṇa,* and also being true to his word, he is another deity of *dharma,* the *apara-dharma-devatā.* This is Lord Rāma, the one who is born in the Ikṣvāku *vaṁśa,* and the first son of Daśaratha. Daśaratha wanted to enthrone him. Thus, Nārada continues to unfold the story of Rāma in a nutshell.

We do not worry whether Rāma is a historical figure. If he is not historical, he is the Lord, we look upon him as an embodiment of *dharma*. *Rāmaḥ vigrahavān dharmaḥ*. Historcially, he is a king, a *rājā*, and so on, who sets a way of life to be lived. Bhārata is a *puṇya-bhūmi* because Rāma walked upon it. This attitude rules the hearts of *Bhāratīyas*.

Śivarātri

Śivarātri falls on the 14th day of the dark fortnight, *kṛṣṇapakṣa,* during the month of *phālguna* (February-March). It is a day dedicated to prayer. On *Śivarātri,* you remain awake the whole night in prayer. The day is spent in *japa,* chanting the names of the Lord like *oṁ namaḥ śivāya.* In Śiva temples elaborate ritual of worship is done the whole day and night.

Certain times are highly auspicious for religious rituals, *mantra-japa,* etc. Based mostly upon the planetary positions, this particular day every year is looked upon as a day of initiation, religious and spiritual. This is the day when the spiritual seekers get *mantra-dīkṣā* and *sannyāsa.* People who are initiated potentise their *mantras*, chanting the *mantras* through the day and night. The *mantras* that they use are spiritual and religious ones. (The *mantras* that are meant to reduce the poison of snakebites, scorpion stings and so on are potentised during the period of solar and lunar eclipses). The planetary positions create an astrologically beneficial condition for spiritual and religious pursuits.

Lord Śiva is auspiciousness

Oṁ namaḥ śivāya, salutation to Lord Śiva. Śiva is *maṅgala,* the ultimate end. Śiva is *mokṣasvarūpa* and *śiva-prāptiḥ* means gain of *mokṣa.* The one who is responsible for creation, sustenance and resolution, *sṛṣṭi, stithi,* and *laya,* and who remains at the same time unsullied, *śuddha,* is Śiva. Unto that Lord, I offer my *namaskāra.*

Let us look at some of the names of Lord Śiva in the *Śivāṣṭottaraśata-nāmāvali* that we chant during *śiva-pūjā. Andhakāsurasūdanāya namaḥ.* Every *ahaṅkāra* is Andhakāsura, an *asura* that causes blindness. The *ahaṅkāra* due to blindness of ignorance does not see things as they are. To the destroyer of that blindness, *sūdanāya,* my salutation, *namaḥ.* Andhakāsura was destroyed by Lord Śiva and given some kind of *mokṣa* from the demonic deeds. Whenever a demon is destroyed, he gets a relative form of *mokṣa.* He is liberated from that demonic nature. This destruction is nothing but the destruction of ignorance, *ajñāna* or *ahaṅkāra.*

Lord Śiva is the lord of time

Kālakālāya namaḥ. Kālasyāpi kālaḥ. Kāla is time or Lord Yama. The Lord of death is called Yama, the *devatā* of time. *Kālakāla* is the one who is Yama to Lord Yama himself, one who is not subject to death. There is a story of a childless couple, told in this context. Sage Mṛgaṇḍu, was a great devotee of Lord Śiva. He prayed to the Lord. Before blessing him with a child, the Lord appeared in the form in which he was invoked. Lord Śiva is *āśutoṣi,* the one who is easily pleased. He said, "I will give you one of two choices. Either you choose to have a son who will live 100 years but be an idiot, or you choose to have a brilliant *sādhu*-son who will live only for 16 years." What a choice! He had no choice, but to take the child who will live for 16 years. This child was called Mārkaṇḍeya.

As expected, the child grew up very well. He studied all the Vedas very quickly, had amazing *medhā-śakti,* and was brilliant. He was also a great devotee of Lord Śiva. The dreaded sixteenth year came. Lord Yama sent his messengers to bring Mārkaṇḍeya. *Yamayati iti yamaḥ,* the one who disciplines everyone is Yama. Lord Yama's domain is all-pervasive, and any object in time is subject to Lord Yama. On that particular day, Mārkaṇḍeya was in the shrine of Lord Śiva, doing *pūjā* to the *śivaliṅgam.* The *liṅga* is a representative form that is meant to include all forms. When Lord Yama's messengers arrived, Mārkaṇḍeya was doing *pūjā* in the temple. The minions of Lord Yama use the *pāśa,* a celestial noose, to claim the soul.

They cannot, however, enter the main shrine to take away any soul. They could not get to Mārkaṇḍeya and wanted him to come out of the shrine. Mārkaṇḍeya decided to stay in the shrine knowing that his time was up. The *dūta*s told Lord Yama that they could not do the job. Lord Yama then tried to get him out, but he would not come out. Therefore, he entered the shrine. Mārkaṇḍeya held on to the *liṅgam* in an embrace. In order to get him, Lord Yama had to take him along with the *liṅga*. He threw his *pāśa*, rope, and pulled Mārkaṇḍeya along with the *liṅga*. Out came the Lord from the *liṅga*. He opened his third eye and Lord Yama was reduced to ashes. The third eye of the Lord, mentioned in *lalāṭākṣāya namaḥ*, means the eye of wisdom. After prayers, Lord Yama was revived and Mārkaṇḍeya became eternal.

Like Āñjaneya, Mārkaṇḍeya is one of the *cirañjīvi*s, the people who never die. He and Lord Śiva became one. As long as you are away from the Lord, you are in the hands of *mṛtyu*, death. If you are not separate from him, you are free from death, time. The Lord of the Lord of time, is *kālakāla*. While Lord Yama destroys everything, the Lord destroys Yama or time.

When you look upon oneself as being time bound, surrender of *ahaṅkāra* is not possible. The *ahaṅkāra* cannot be surrendered because to surrender it, you need to objectify it, which means you need to be outside of it. It is the *ahaṅkāra* that does the offering. You can surrender everything else, but you will remain. Only one thing can destroy the *ahaṅkāra* and that is knowledge born of *śāstra*, which makes you see that there is only Īśvara. Then there is enlightened *ahaṅkāra*. This is the end of all pursuits.

Gurupūrṇimā

Just as you have Father's Day and Mother's Day, *Gurupūrṇimā* is *guru*'s day. This is also called *vyāsa-pūrṇimā*, the anniversary of Bhagavān Vyāsa who occupies an exalted place in the hierarchy of teachers. Although there were also *guru*s for Veda Vyāsa, we look upon Veda Vyāsa as the link between the teachers that we know and the teachers that we do not know.

Cāturmāsya-vrata

On this particular day, the *sannyāsin*s make a *vrata*, a vow, to stay in one place and teach for two months. *Gurupūrṇimā* occurs at the beginning of the rainy season in India, during which time one finds many small insects on the ground. At the time of taking *sannyāsa*, one takes a vow of not hurting any living being. In order to avoid killing even small insects on their path, the *sannyāsin*s do not travel during these two months, starting from *Gurupūrṇimā* day. Even though they usually travel from place to place, they stay in one place during this period and teach. Traditionally, the place they choose is located in an area between two rivers, or between a river and a stream. They move within the area, without crossing the river or streams.

The vow is called *cāturmāsya-vrata*. A *māsa* is a month or a fortnight—*pakṣo vai māsaḥ iti*. So, a vow for two months is called *cāturmāsyam*, four fortnights.

On this day of *Gurupūrṇimā*, the start of *cāturmāsyam*, they invoke the *guruparaṁparā*, the lineage of teachers in the tradition, especially in *maṭha*s, monastic places of learning.

There are many *maṭha*s, including the *śaṅkara-maṭha*s. The head of each *maṭha* is like a pontiff, and has a certain following. Each one of these heads performs a daily *pūjā* to invoke the *guru*s in the hierarchy. There are at least 16 *guru*s in the *paraṁparā*, and the grace of each is invoked in a vessel containing water. That is the ritual aspect of it.

A guru unfolds spiritual knowledge

The word '*guru*' has a number of meanings. The one who teaches is a *guru*; the one who advises is also a *guru*. These days, the word '*guru*' is also used in the English language. In the American press, we find '*guru*' being used very widely by journalists. They say, for instance, 'He is an automobile *guru*,' or 'He is a stock market *guru*.' Even in India, it is used in that way. When I was a boy, I wanted to learn a very complex form of martial art in which a stick is used. It is an excellent discipline that teaches coordination and other skills. One of our family's farm workers was a teacher of this art. When I asked him to teach me, he said that I had to come to him with *gurudakṣiṇā*, the traditional offering to the teacher. I gave him a coconut, fruits, flowers, and a small amount of money. Only then would he begin teaching. His respect for his art was so great that he called himself a *guru*, and I respected him as such. When a person thinks of himself or herself as a *guru*, the one who learns from him or her also feels the same way. He or she evokes in you the feeling of a disciple. In addition to martial art teachers, classical dance masters and musicians also insist on being called *guru*s. Many teachers of art-forms that must be taught directly are considered *guru*s.

While I have nothing against such usage, the word '*guru*' really can be used only for a person who imparts spiritual knowledge. A *guru* is one who unfolds the knowledge that you are the whole, non-separate from the Lord. A *guru* is the *upadeśa-kartṛ*, one who is the teacher of the *mahā-vākya*, the equation revealing that you are the whole.

The wholeness, which you seek, is not separate from you. The very seeking is because the whole is you; you want to be yourself. The one who teaches that is a *guru*. That is the final definition. He is the *mahāvākya-upadeśa-kartṛ*, the one who teaches the statement revealing the identity of the individual in relation to the Lord, the whole.

We invoke the Lord in the guru

The *guru* is a human being. When the *guru* is praised, however, as in the following verse, the human element is not taken into account.

गुरुर्ब्रह्मा गुरुर्विष्णुः गुरुर्देवो महेश्वरः ।
गुरुरेव परं ब्रह्म तस्मै श्रीगुरवे नमः ॥

gururbrahmā gururviṣṇuḥ gururdevo maheśvaraḥ,
gurureva paraṁ brahma tasmai śrīgurave namaḥ.

The *guru* is Brahmā, the *guru* is Viṣṇu, the *guru* is Maheśvara (Śiva), the *guru* is the self-revealing limitless Brahman. Salutations to that revered *guru*.

Only the truth element is taken into account because the *guru* teaches that you are Brahman, you are limitless. When he teaches that you are limitless, he does not mean, "I am limited; you are limitless." In fact, you are limitless and he is limitless.

The limitless is Brahmā, the limitless is Viṣṇu, the limitless is Rudra, or Śiva, and the limitless is you. Everything is this limitless Brahman. So, when we praise the *guru*, the human element is just completely absorbed in the total. You either relegate the human element to the background, or you absorb it into the total. It is the total that is worshipped. In that way, the *guru*, the person with a human body who teaches, becomes a kind of an altar of worship, but what is being invoked is the Lord. When you worship the form of Śrī Dakṣiṇāmūrti in the temple, it is not the form you are worshipping, but the Lord. You invoke and worship the Lord in a particular form. Similarly, when you praise the person who teaches you and for whom you have *śraddhā*, it is not the individual person you praise, but the teaching itself, for what he teaches is not separate from him.

Praise of the *guru* is praise for the truth of the teaching.

अखण्डमण्डलाकारं व्याप्तं येन चराचरम्।
तत्पदं दर्शितं येन तस्मै श्रीगुरवे नमः॥

akhaṇḍamaṇḍalākāraṁ vyāptaṁ yena
carācaram,
tatpadaṁ darśitaṁ yena tasmai
śrīgurave namaḥ.

My salutations unto that *guru* who showed
me the abode of the one who is to be known,

> whose form is the entire universe and, by who pervades all that moves and all that does not move.

Tasmai śrīgurave namaḥ, unto that *guru*, my *namaskāra*, my salutation; *tatpadaṁ darśitaṁ yena*, by whom that *pada*, that end or abode, was shown very clearly, *darśitam*. And what is that *pada? Yena padena carācaraṁ vyāptam*, by which *pada* the whole universe is pervaded. Here, *pada* is Brahman. *Yena*, by which Brahman, this entire universe, *akhaṇḍa-maṇḍalākāram*, of living beings and inert things, *carācaram*, is pervaded, *vyāptam*. My salutations to the teacher who has shown me the Lord (the *vastu*, the reality) in the form of this great universe.

The gaining of any knowledge is the greatest miracle. How is the mind able to grasp a new fact or concept? If you are ignorant by nature, you cannot know and if you know by nature, you need not be taught. The fact is that you cannot see more than you know, yet you keep increasing your existing knowledge; you keep on shedding ignorance. That is because under certain conditions you are able to see. The teacher is the one who creates those conditions. He does so by using reason and by citing your own experiences. In that way, he helps you see. In fact, the teacher creates an inner environment in which you cannot but see. That is what teaching is about. It is a miracle, an impossibility that happens.

You cannot see more than you already know; yet you always do. That is how you know more and more. How can that happen? The answer is very simple: you are all-knowledge.

We say that the Lord is all-knowledge; that all-knowledge is in the Lord. Yet, who is this Lord? If the Lord were to say, "I am the Lord," that 'I am' is not going to be any different from the meaning of the statement 'I am'. When you say, 'I am,' it is exactly the same as the 'I am' of the Lord. There is one limitless consciousness. Consciousness cannot be limited because it is one, and it is formless. The Lord is a conscious being, and the limitless consciousness is the same for the Lord and for you. You are limited only with reference to your body, mind and sense organs. As consciousness, you are limitless. The Lord is also limitless consciousness. Being limitless, there is only one consciousness. If the Lord is all-knowledge, that all-knowledge rests in the consciousness that is one, that is limitless, that is you. This means that all-knowledge rests in you.

Knowing implies removal of inhibiting factors

If all-knowledge rests in me, why don't I know everything? With reference to the individual, the knowledge is inhibited. With reference to the Lord, it is uninhibited. This inhibiting factor is what we call *āvaraṇa*, something that covers knowledge. When we create the conditions for knowledge to take place, the *āvaraṇa* goes away. That *āvaraṇa*, veiling, vanishes, so that knowledge is unveiled. Interestingly, the English word that refers to any new finding is 'discovery'—dispelling the cover, dismissing the cover. Whether intentionally coined in that way, the word is amazingly apt. The cover is the veil—*āvaraṇa*. Knowledge needs only be uncovered because it is already there. Any knowledge is only from the Lord, whether it is the knowledge of how to make *pizza* or the knowledge of a quantum object. Every form of knowledge is in the all-knowledge. The removal of the inhibiting factor is what we call knowing. Like a surgeon who removes cataract so that you can see the world, the *guru* creates the conditions for ignorance to be dispelled, so that you can see the truth of yourself and the world.

There are two types of blindness. One is not treatable; the other is. As an example to the process of knowing, this second type of blindness is pointed out in the following verse:

अज्ञानतिमिरान्धस्य ज्ञानाञ्जनशलाकया ।
चक्षुरुन्मीलितं येन तस्मै श्रीगुरवे नमः ॥

ajñānatimirāndhasya jñānāñjanaśalākayā,
cakṣurunmīlitaṁ yena
tasmai śrīgurave namaḥ.

My salutation to that *guru* by whom the eye (of knowledge) is opened for the one who is blind due to ignorance by applying the ointment of knowledge.

Here, the example is a blind person, *andha*. What is the cause of the blindness? *Timira*, cataract. Due to cataract, the person is not able to see; he is *timira-andha*. What is to be done? The surgeon removes the cataract. In India, in the days in which this verse was composed, they seem to have had a remedy in the form of an ointment to remove cataract. *Añjana* means ointment. *Añjana-śalākayā*, by applying this ointment, the problem was solved. So too, here, even though you are a knowing person, essentially an all-knowledge person, that knowledge is covered by ignorance. Therefore, everybody is *ajñāna-timira-andha*, blind due to the cataract of ignorance. Ignorance alone is the cataract because of which one becomes blind, *ajñānam eva timiraṁ tena timireṇa andhaḥ bhavati*. This ignorance alone is the *timira*, the cataract, because of which knowledge is inhibited. Unto him, *tasmai*, by whom, *yena*, that inhibiting factor is removed, the inner eye of knowledge, *cakṣuḥ*, is opened, *unmīlitam*, my *namaskāra*. Therefore, the *guru* does not really 'deliver' anything. He just removes that inhibiting factor and helps you see. It is a highly responsible job. So the one who knows the truth and the method of teaching it, can only do it. If the teacher doesn't know, he will only confuse others with his words.

In one text, it is said that the *guru* must be a person with an ounce of extra compassion. Ordinary compassion is not enough. Any human being will have empathy when one sees a person in pain. He may begin helping him or her in whichever way he can. That is natural human compassion. However, if one sees someone suffering for no reason at all, empathy-born compassion will not be evoked. It is through the gate of empathy that compassion and the desire to help are evoked. Since a person who suffers for no reason may not evoke empathy, it takes someone with extra compassion to choose to help that person.

Let us suppose this man mistakenly believes that a snake has bitten him. If a snake has really bitten him, you could help him by taking him to the hospital for an anti-venom injection. Perhaps you could even administer first aid by tying a piece of cloth above the bite and making an opening for the poisoned blood to escape. These are the practical steps that you could take, all of which are induced by your empathy. But what can you do for the *ajñāna-sarpadaṣṭa* when he screams, "help! help! I've been bitten by a snake!" When you ask him where he was bitten, he points to his foot, saying, "There!" He refuses to even look in the direction of what he feels to be a deadly wound. However, when you look at his foot, you see only a thorn lodged there, which you remove. You ask, "Do you feel better now?" you ask. "No, no!" he cries. "I was bitten by a snake!" In fact, he merely stepped on a thorn, and when he looked down near his foot he saw a water hose. His panic has created a snake out of the hose and deadly fangs out of the thorn. He manifests all the effects of fear, sweating, pounding heart and he may even die of fright, merely due to his belief, "I was bitten by the snake!" True or not, since he thinks so, it is true for him. Yet, knowing that he is not in danger, you cannot help but feel some amusement, rather than empathy.

So, how will you help this person? Since there is no danger, you could walk away, but still, you see how he is suffering. Which is why an extra ounce of compassion is required. That compassion comes from the realisation, "I was once like that; I went through that experience, too." If I had gone through the same blessed thing, I can easily appreciate the person's lot and I can be of help. That is why the *guru* is described as *ahetuka-dayāsindhuḥ*—an ocean of *dayā*, compassion, without any reason. There is no reason. The student may ask, "Why are you so compassionate? Why should you teach me at all? What have I done?" "Nothing." "What do you expect of me?" "Nothing." You ask why I teach you. "Why should I not teach you? You need to be taught, so I teach."

The teaching method

A teaching method is required because the problem is a very peculiar one. This knowledge is not like a given academic subject that you can learn simply by reading a textbook. It is a complete unfolding and the teacher-student connection is necessary in order to make the knowledge work for the student. It is similar to a relationship with a therapist in which trust and certain amount of time are necessary. The *guru* is more like a super-therapist. He must re-orient the student over a period of time, directly or indirectly, so that the student sees through the fallacy of his or her ingrained self-beliefs, and help the person see that the self is totally acceptable.

In experiential love, you have that kind of feeling, because when somebody says, "I love you," you feel totally and unconditionally accepted. Everything about you, your height, your nose, and your mind, is accepted. That experience gives you an inner opening to see that you are acceptable, at least to one other person. It is not real self-acceptance because it is based on the others' approval of you. You think you are okay only because the other person says, "I love you." The approval does not come through your own eyes but from the eyes of the other. Later on, you may both discover a lot of things about each other that are not acceptable at all. Then you find the other person is adding clauses to "I love you." "I love you even though..." "I would be happy loving you if you could get up a little earlier, if you could think a little differently, if you were not a Republican..." Afterwards you tack on conditions, and the unconditional acceptance that you need is not gained through the eyes of others. Since you do not feel totally acceptable in your own eyes, you go on seeking it in the eyes of others.

That is why it is so very important to have an insight about you as totally lovable and acceptable. That is what the *guru* does; he helps you see yourself as lovable. He frees you. Then that vision is yours, and you become a source of love to everyone else. That is why the *guru-śiṣya* relationship is entirely different from any other relationship and the reason why the *guru* is given so much praise in the *śāstra* and in the tradition.

Gurupūrṇimā is, thus, a very important day for all seekers. On this *Guru*'s day, we seek the blessings of all the *guru*s in the *paraṁparā*, the tradition, bearing in mind that the ultimate *guru* is Lord Dakṣiṇāmūrti, the source of all knowledge. Therefore, we praise him, and worship him, seeking the grace of the *guru*.

Śrī Śaṅkara Jayanti

To talk about Śrī Śaṅkarācārya is to unfold Īśvara, the Lord. We do not look upon Śrī Śaṅkara as an individual. In fact, we do not look upon any teacher as an individual. When he is not a person, there cannot be *jayanti* or birthday celebration either. We do not have an *īśvara-jayanti*, while we do have *Rāma-navamī* and *Kṛṣṇa-aṣṭamī*.

Even though Īśvara is in the form of Lord Rāma and Śrī Kṛṣṇa, the particular form of Lord Rāma or Śrī Kṛṣṇa has a history. These forms appeared as *avatāra*s at a given time and disappeared at a given time. Yet they can be worshipped as Īśvara. Every form, no doubt, is Īśvara's form, but Īśvara in the form of Śrī Rāma or Kṛṣṇa is someone with whom I can relate, and at whose feet I can place a flower. The form can become an altar where I can offer worship. The forms of Śrī Kṛṣṇa and Lord Rāma are available for worship and contemplation as the Lord. That is why we celebrate *Rāma-navamī*, and *Kṛṣṇa-aṣṭamī*.

When Śrī Kṛṣṇa uses the first person singular in the *Bhagavad Gītā*, it is only in the sense of his being Īśvara. Īśvara who is limitless, the *vastu*, upon taking a given form, *upādhi*, becomes the *avatāra*. Similarly, to think of the birth of Śrī Śaṅkara is possible only from the standpoint of the *upādhi*. From this standpoint alone is a *jayanti* possible.

A *guru* is always looked upon as the very vision that he teaches. That is the difference between what Śrī Śaṅkara taught and what any other teacher would teach. If a teacher teaches: 'Īśvara is Īśvara, *jagat* is *jagat*, and you are what you are,' what will you feel after listening to such a teacher? You knew this very well even before you went to the teacher. This was your thinking when you went to the teacher, and were exposed to the *upaniṣads*. How can it be that you feel the same way afterwards? You will definitely conclude that the teacher cannot be the *vastu* since he teaches that the *vastu* is different from you, and even him.

If the teacher says that you are the *vastu*, then the teacher is the same *vastu*. If he teaches about the one *vastu* that there is, he can be looked upon as the very *vastu* itself. That is why we say that the *guru* in the form of the *vastu* alone is Brahmā, that alone is Viṣṇu, and that alone is Īśvara, Maheśvara. The Trinity is nothing but the *vastu*. You are also the same *vastu*. The one who teaches this is not separate from the *vastu*.

In the *guru*, you have an *upādhi* talking about *vastu*, which is not in any way limited by the *upādhi*. The *upādhi* is limited by time, limited by place, and limited by its own accomplishments. In spite of this, the *upādhi* does not limit the *vastu*. An individual who has understood this is as good as Śrī Śaṅkara himself.

Śrī Śaṅkarācārya as upādhi-viśeṣa

There have been many enlightened teachers in the world besides Veda Vyāsa who compiled all the Vedas and wrote the *Brahma-sūtras*, and Śrī Śaṅkara who made the knowledge available to the common people. Only some of them are remembered and not others. Why do we worship only Veda Vyāsa and Śrī Śaṅkara and not the others? If some other teacher is talking about the same thing when he says, "You are not separate from the *vastu*," what is so special about Veda Vyāsa and Śrī Śaṅkara?

A person is remembered with respect in history because of a significant contribution he or she made to the contemporary society, which proves often to be a blessing for future generations. Therefore, he or she becomes a very special person; an *upādhi-viśeṣa*.

Upādhi-viśeṣa can also mean that a particular person has some special features or miraculous capacity. Generally, anyone having miraculous powers is praised. However, Hindu tradition does not have an exaggerated value for miracles; they are not considered noteworthy. If you look at the tradition, you will find that the *asuras* had miraculous powers and performed various tricks. We find that every *asura* in the *Mahābhārata* had these powers. It was also possible for an *asura* to assume another form.

In the *Rāmāyaṇa*, Mārīca came in the form of a deer. Some individuals can be carried away by miracles, but in the Hindu tradition, these types of miracles have no real meaning. Hindus are traditionally not miracle-mongers because having the power to perform miracles was common. The *asura*s were *niśācara*s, those who moved in the night, and *khecara*s, those who moved in the sky. All these had *upādhi-viśeṣa*. If a performer of miracles were to be worshipped, the *asuras* could not have been destroyed!

People of mediocre knowledge think of a great man only as a miracle performer. For instance, some of them extol the *Kanakadhārā Stotram*. This is the story of Śrī Śaṅkara's bringing forth a shower of gold coins for the poor woman who gave him a berry when he went to her house for alms. However, when we praise Śrī Śaṅkara we neither consider nor are we interested in the miracles attributed to him. There is a verse we generally repeat whenever we think of Śrī Śaṅkara that reveals how Śrī Śaṅkara is *upādhi-viśeṣa*.

श्रुतिस्मृतिपुराणानामालयं करुणालयम् ।
नमामि भगवत्पादं शङ्करं लोकशङ्करम् ॥

śrutismṛtipurāṇānām ālayaṁ karuṇālayam,
namāmi bhagavatpādaṁ śaṅkaraṁ lokaśaṅkaram.

I bow at the feet of the Lord in the form of Śrī Śaṅkarācārya, who is the blessing for the humanity, who is the shrine for the *śruti*, the *smṛti* and the *purāṇa*, and, who is the abode of compassion.

In this verse, there is a statement of fact: Śrī Śaṅkara is *śrutismṛtipurāṇānām ālayam*. A shrine, a temple, is called *ālaya*. Also any place where a sacred thing is kept is an *ālaya*. Books are sacred, so a library is called *pustakālaya*. Śrī Śaṅkarācārya is an *ālaya* of *śruti-smṛti-purāṇa*s. *Śruti* is all the Vedas, the *karmakāṇḍa* as well as the last portion of the Vedas known as Vedanta. Since *śruti* has come down to us through the *ṛṣi*s, there is no authorship, whereas, *smṛti* has authorship. The *kalpa-sūtra*s are a development of the statements of the *smṛti*, written by people who had a status similar to the one the *ṛṣi*s enjoyed. They knew about rituals, values, *dharma*, etc. All the *dharma-śāstra*s come under *smṛti*. Even *itihāsa* is called *smṛti*. It is a combination of history and poetry, unlike Indian history, that is half history and half fiction! The *purāṇa* appears on a bigger canvas. Its topic is entirely different. It talks about Bhagavān's *avatāra*s. There are 18 *purāṇa*s. All these together abide in one shrine that is Śrī Śaṅkara. He is the *upādhi* in which the entire subject matter of the *śruti*, *smṛti* and *purāṇa*s is enshrined, and is therefore called *śrutismṛtipurāṇānām ālayam*.

Suppose, there is a living person who is an embodiment of all this vast knowledge but is a *maunibaba*, a person committed to silence, not talking or writing, what would we get? There would be no way for us to learn anything from him. *Maunibaba*s are always respected in our country. If Śrī Śaṅkara had been such a *maunibaba*, he might have had many devotees and one or two generations of those devotees might have remembered him. However, we definitely would not be celebrating his *jayanti*. Śrī Śaṅkara was not only an *ālaya* of all-knowledge, but also an *ālaya* of *karuṇā*, a person of great compassion through which he was able to reach out to others. It was Śrī Śaṅkara's compassion, which made him what he was.

Śrī Śaṅkara taught his disciples who were with him, but he also made sure that the teaching came down to posterity through his writings. In those days, writing was not an easy job. There were no typewriters; there were no laptops, or even paper and pens. Śrī Śaṅkara had to do all his writing on palm leaves, and every copy was handwritten. There are hundreds of such manuscripts in India today, in spite of so many of them having been burnt or lost. They are enshrined in the homes of the people who have them. I do not think there is any culture other than Vedic culture that accords so much value to learning, whether it is scriptural or temporal.

Śrī Śaṅkara wrote extensive commentaries, *bhāṣya*s, on the *Īśa, Kena, Kaṭha, Praśna, Muṇḍaka, Māṇḍūkya, Taittirīya, Aitareya, Chāndogya* and the *Bṛhadāraṇyaka Upaniṣad*s. All these *bhāṣya*s were written to include *pūrvapakṣa*s, objections and arguments, and the unfolding of the *siddhānta*, main purport. When writing *bhāṣya*s, first, you have to give the *anvaya*, comprehensive meaning. After that, you should defend this analysis against any other possible meaning, or any other meaning given by somebody else. If one person thinks in one way, there will always be another person who thinks differently. People say that there are different schools of thought. When you are dealing with the reality, it has to be dealt with exactly as it is. There cannot be different schools of thought in arithmetic because one plus one can only be two. How can there be 'schools of thought' in understanding Īśvara? But there were people who looked at Īśvara differently. Śaṅkara valued them all and discussed in detail leaving nothing to be desired.

You can give people the freedom to hold their ideas. There is nothing wrong in that, but there is no way of reconciling what is right with whatever is wrong. What is right is right. There is nothing to reconcile. A wrong thing has to be stated as wrong and understood as such. The other person has the freedom to hold a wrong idea. That is understandable. However, you cannot accept this wrong idea just because he is a nice person. You cannot have a charismatic approach in dealing with realities.

We can imagine the enormity of effort in writing all this on palm leaves. How much compassion

Śrī Śaṅkara must have had for the spiritual upliftment of humanity, that he wrote all these books, and finally, the *Brahma-sūtra-bhāṣya*. It is no ordinary feat. This is the proof of his compassion. Therefore, he is called *śrutismṛtipurāṇānāṁ ālayam karuṇālayam*.

Namāmi bhagavatpādaṁ śaṅkaraṁ lokaśaṅkaram. I salute him whose name is Śrī Śaṅkara. *Śaṁ karoti iti śaṅkaraḥ*. Śaṅkara is he who grants *maṅgalam*, an auspicious end, the grand finale to the winding journey of a *jīva*. The *jīva*'s history has to end. When will it end? Each birth is like yet another sheet of paper in a set of loose sheets that can never be bound together. It is endless; there is always a next birth. It is always an unbound book. The one who brings about that *maṅgalam* is Śaṅkara Bhagavatpāda, who is likened to Bhagavān. Unto him, my *namaskāra*. Is there any miracle pointed out in this verse?

Śrī Śaṅkarācārya and the teaching tradition, sampradāya

Veda Vyāsa wrote the *sūtra*s and Śrī Śaṅkara wrote the *bhāṣya* on the *sūtra*s. One was, thus, the *sūtra-kṛt*, and the other, the *bhāṣya-kṛt*. They made the *sampradāya*, tradition available in the form of the written word, and successive teachers have drawn their teaching from this. The following is a verse that is chanted in paying our respects to Śrī Śaṅkara and Veda Vyāsa.

शङ्करं शङ्कराचार्यं केशवं बादरायणम् ।
सूत्रभाष्यकृतौ वन्दे भगवन्तौ पुनः पुनः ॥

śaṅkaraṁ śaṅkarācāryaṁ keśavaṁ bādarāyaṇam, sūtrabhāṣyakṛtau vande bhagavantau punaḥ punaḥ.

Salutations again and again to Lord Śiva in the form of Śrī Śaṅkarācārya and Lord Viṣṇu in the form of Veda Vyāsa, who were the authors of *sūtra* and *bhāṣya*.

Śrī Śaṅkara presents the very method of teaching in his commentary. Even though there is no discussion exclusively dealing with the method of teaching in his *bhāṣya*, Śaṅkara employs the method. We learn how to present a subject-matter, how to expand it and how a word is to be unfolded, how do we come to know exactly what the *śruti* says in a given sentence—it is for all this that you require a *sampradāya*. Śrī Śaṅkara says that a teacher should be a *sampradāya-vit*, a knower of the teaching tradition. He says,[24] *asampradāyavid mūrkhavad upekṣaṇīyaḥ*, just as one keeps away from a *mūrkha*, an uninformed person who seriously debates, one has to keep away from *asampradāyavit*. Śrī Śaṅkara identifies with the *sampradāya* and reveals himself as a *sampradāya-vit*.

---

[24] *Bhagavad Gītā Bhāṣya* 13.2

It is also necessary for us to see Śrī Śaṅkara as a *sampradāya-kṛt,* one who creates and maintains the tradition. He did not say that. It was not necessary for him to do so. Without his revealing the *sampradāya* through his own *bhāṣya,* there would have been no way for us to approach the *śruti* and get the vision. In the second chapter of the *Brahmasūtra-bhāṣya,* he deals with the various schools of thought and points out their errors. In doing so, he also reveals himself as a *sampradāya-kṛt* in a way. Therefore, Śrī Śaṅkara is looked upon as a link in the *sampradāya.*

Many people wrote commentaries on Śrī Śaṅkara's *bhāṣya* to further their own understanding and clarity. We thus have many commentaries available. Some of them are popular. We need not read them all, but they are useful. These commentaries help us in understanding the original.

This wisdom helps one understand that the truth is above all perceived differences. In this, it helps one to become more accommodative of all differences. It is not an accommodation with a patronising attitude, but born of understanding from where the perceptions come. In a healthy dialogue they can be resolved.

Śrī Śaṅkara's teaching is a blessing to humanity, which is now struggling to cope with the problems of differences. *Vande punaḥ punaḥ.* To that Śrī Śaṅkarācārya, I offer my salutation again, and again.

Oṁ tat sat

Books by Swami Dayananda Saraswati

Public Talk Series :

1. Living Intelligently
2. Need for Cognitive Change
3. Discovering Love
4. Successful Living
5. The Value of Values
6. Vedic View and Way of Life

Upaniṣad Series :

7. Muṇḍakopaniṣad
8. Kenopaniṣad

Moments with Oneself Series :

9. Freedom from Helplessness
10. Living versus Getting On
11. Insights
12. Action and Reaction
13. The Fundamental Problem
14. Problem is You, Solution is You
15. Purpose of Prayer
16. Vedanta 24x7
17. Freedom
18. Crisis Management
19. Surrender and Freedom
20. The Need for Personal Reorganisation
21. Freedom in Relationship
22. Stress-free Living

Text Translation Series :

23. Śrīmad Bhagavad Gītā
    (Text with roman transliteration and English translation)

Stotra Series :

24. Dipārādhanā
25. Prayer Guide
    (With explanations of several Mantras, Stotras, Kirtans and Religious Festivals)

Exploring Vedanta Series : (*vākyavicāra*)

26. śraddhā bhakti dhyāna yogād avaihi
    ātmānaṁ ced vijānīyāt

Bhagavad Gītā Series :

27. Bhagavad Gītā Home Study Program
    Vol 1-4 (Hardbound)
28. Bhagavad Gītā Home Study Program
    Vol 1-4 (Softbound)

Essays :

29. Do all Religions have the same goal?
30. Conversion is Violence
31. Gurupūrṇimā
32. Dānam
33. Japa
34. Can We?
35. **Teaching Tradition of Advaita Vedanta**

BOOKS BY SMT. SHEELA BALAJI

36. Salutations to Rudra
    (based on the exposition of Śrī Rudram by Swami Dayananda Saraswati)
37. Without a Second

Also available at :

ARSHA VIDYA RESEARCH
AND PUBLICATION TRUST
32/4 Sir Desika Road
Mylapore Chennai 600 004
Telefax : 044 - 2499 7131
Email : avrandpc@gmail.com

ARSHA VIDYA GURUKULAM
Anaikatti P.O.
Coimbatore 641 108
Ph : 0422 - 2657001
Fax : 0422 - 2657002
Email : office@arshavidya.in

ARSHA VIDYA GURUKULAM
P.O.Box 1059. Pennsylvania
PA 18353, USA.
Ph : 001-570-992-2339
Email : avp@epix.net

SWAMI DAYANANDA ASHRAM
Purani Jhadi, P.B. No. 30
Rishikesh, Uttaranchal 249 201
Telefax : 0135-2430769
Email : ashrambookstore@yahoo.com

AND IN ALL THE LEADING BOOK STORES, INDIA